How to Control Any Conversation

Simple Ways to Deal with Difficult
People and Awkward Situations

Peter W. Murphy

Copyright (C) 2011 by Peter W. Murphy

This publication contains the opinions and ideas of its author and is intended for informational purposes only. While attempts have been made to verify information contained in this publication, neither the author nor the publisher assumes any responsibility for errors, omissions, interpretation or usage of the subject matter herein. The author and publisher shall in no event be held liable for any loss or other damages incurred from the usage of this publication.

Table of Contents

How to Use this Book 5
Free Conversation Skills Training 6

Section 1
Introduction 7
Why is it Important to Take Control? 8
How to Take Control of a Conversation 10
Ways People Lose Control of a Conversation 20
How to Regain Self-Control
      When Someone Disturbs You 26
How to Prepare in Advance to Ensure Success 31
What Skills do You Need to Strengthen
      to Maintain Control? 34

Section 2
52 Conversation Blueprints 36
How to Get People to Admire You 37
How to Get People to Agree with You 39
How to Get People to Answer Your Questions 41
How to Get People to Appreciate You 43
How to Get People to Be Nice to You 46
How to Get People to Be on Time 48
How to Get People to Be Quiet 50
How to Get People to Believe in You 52
How to Get People to Believe You 55
How to Get People to Do What You Say 57
How to Get People to Feel Sorry for You 59
How to Get People to Forgive You 62
How to Get People to Go Away 64
How to Get People to Help You 66
How to Get People to Interact 68
How to Get People to Invite You Places 70

How to Get People to Like You More	72
How to Get People to Listen to You	74
How to Get People to Meet Deadlines	76
How to Get People to Mind Their Own Business	79
How to Get People to Not Make Fun of You	81
How to Get People to Notice You	84
How to Get People to Open Up	87
How to Get People to Pay Attention to You	89
How to Get People to Respect You	91
How to Get People to Shut Up	93
How to Get People to Take You Seriously	95
How to Get People to Talk about Themselves	97
How to Get People to Talk to You	99
How to Get People to Tell the Truth	101
How to Get People to Trust You	104
How to Get People to Understand You	106
How to Get People to Want to Be Around You	108
How to Deal with Difficult People at Home	110
How to Deal with Difficult People at Work	112
How to Deal with Difficult People on the Phone	114
How to Deal with Difficult People in Life	117
How to Deal with Difficult Family Members	119
How to Deal with Angry People	121
How to Deal with Ignorant People	123
How to Deal with Obnoxious People	125
How to Deal with Passive Aggressive People	127
How to Deal with Rude People	130
How to Deal with Selfish People	132
How to Deal with Unreasonable People	134
How to Deal with Verbal Abuse	137
How to Be Less Awkward around People	139
How to Talk without Arguing	141
How to Talk with Confidence	144
How to Talk with New People	146
How to Deal with Loneliness	148
How to Talk with Strangers	150

How to Use this Book

This book is not designed to be read from beginning to end, unlike most self help books. Instead it is designed to be used as a resource you can turn to anytime you face challenges dealing with people, times when you need to take control of the conversations you are having. Dip into the book and pick out what you need rather than sitting down to read the pages and pages of tips at one time.

The book is composed of 52 conversation blueprints. To get the greatest value from these pages use the Table of Contents to go directly to the issue you want to deal with. Then read and apply the tips presented right away.

Another day you might want to focus on a different issue, again, look through the Table of Contents to find what you're looking for and go directly to it.

An important point. Make sure to use these principles and ideas out there in the real world. It may take a little trial and error but if you practice you'll see it's much easier than most people think to control any conversation. You'll have much more fun talking to people and you'll enjoy letting your personality shine.

Do bear in mind, the strategies presented here are a starting point, you'll need to adjust your application of the individual tips to the context and people you are dealing with. Some flexibility on your part is essential.

Take it a step at a time, aim to improve just a little each day, use these strategies often and make a commitment to ongoing learning with the free resources mentioned in the next section. Before long you'll be one of those people others respect and admire. They'll be wondering how you take control of the conversation so easily!

Free Conversation Skills Training

I am a firm believer in ongoing education and for that reason I am including two free bonuses with this book that will help you to build great communication skills.

1. 10 Simple Steps to Communication Confidence

I have a very popular audio that covers the 10 steps to building communication confidence – that magnetic quality that makes people want to talk to you and keen to get to know you better.

If you'd like to know how to win the approval, admiration and deep appreciation of anyone you talk to then you'll enjoy listening to this special recording.

This special audio has been downloaded several thousand times over the last few years. Get your free copy at: http://www.FreeNowToday.com/

2. Communication Confidence Blog

My blog has hundreds of great articles with practical tips for anyone interested in developing better communication skills, overcoming shyness or building lasting self confidence. You can even add your own comments to let me know what you think.
http://www.HowToTalkWithConfidence.com/blog/

3. Follow Me on Twitter

For personal development tweets – new insights, discoveries you can use and interesting news.
https://twitter.com/#!/MurphyPeterW

4. Amazon.com Author page

To see my biography, visit my author page at Amazon.com:
https://www.amazon.com/author/peterwmurphy

Section 1

Introduction

Taking control of a conversation simply means you direct the flow of the conversation in order to achieve a specific desired outcome, whether that is an agreement, harmony between all participants, or simply to maintain a positive tone throughout. It does not mean dominating the conversation or verbally "beating" your opponent(s).

What is the best way to take control of a conversation? That's something I've been asked many times and why I released this book to give you empowering tools which will enable you to assume control of any conversation and achieve your goal for that conversation. It's something that you will find definitely improves with practice, so I encourage you to practice doing this, every chance you get! Even when making small talk, try out the techniques and observe how much easier it gets, and how much more comfortable you become at taking control.

While there's really no tried and true, "works every time like a charm" silver bullet promise I can make you about successfully controlling each and every conversation immediately, I am happy to share with you some basic tenets that do, indeed, work – and work well. Practice makes perfect, remember – so once you have mastered these fundamental principles, you'll find yourself subtly yet masterfully directing any conversation about any topic, even when that involves a variety of people and their differing personality types.

I have refined these fundamentals after years of practice and trial and error. I've been fortunate enough to have observed some true masters of conversation control over those years – folks who are so good at it, most people have no clue that they've handed over the reins of the conversation willingly and happily. And now you can learn to do this, too!

Why is it Important to Take Control?

It's possible to come up with any number of reasons why taking control of a conversation should be viewed as important. Oftentimes, it depends upon the situation.

For instance, let's say you're someone who tends to feel overpowered by a talking dynamo of the opposite sex. You know, you tend to just throw in several "uh-huhs" where you feel they're appropriate, because that's about all the fast-talking other party is allowing you to do! Don't be intimidated or allow yourself to be railroaded into listening (not conversing) to something you're not even remotely interested in.

If you're worried about being perceived as rude by not listening to them go on and on about something that's not the least bit intriguing to you, consider this – it's actually ruder to pretend to care about that topic, and mislead them into thinking you might like to go to the next miniature dollhouse convention that comes to town! (Or whatever they've been going on and on about that has been creating a great cure for insomnia from your perspective).

Now, that's not to say that you shouldn't care what the other person has to say – not at all. But if you really have no input other than "uh-huh" now and again, it's not really a conversation, is it? Letting it go on and on ad nauseam really serves no purpose, other than to drain your energy and waste your time. Taking control of this type of pseudo-conversation and turning it into a real one is a valuable skill, and well worth cultivating.

In a scenario like the one just described, you can actually get a word in edgewise by interjecting a question, and then gradually maneuvering the conversation in the direction you'd prefer. In other words, to convert this to an actual two-way communication, you might (at a key point) say, "Oh, wow! I remember feeling that way once. There's a movie I love that made that point so well. Have you ever seen Hereafter?" If the response is "no," you have the perfect opportunity to explain the plot briefly, and switch the subject to one that you actually will enjoy. Or even to get the other person talking about movies in general, if that's something that you find more interesting than their first topic. Or choose a book, or piece of music that you really love, so you are shifting gears toward something about which you are comfortable, confident and interested. If the other person is someone you'd like to get to know better, this is also a great way to discover some common ground, for future conversations.

Let's look at a different situation. If you've ever applied for a loan at a bank, you know how nervous that can make you feel. Especially with the current economic downturn, and credit needing to be even more exemplary than ever before, in order to obtain a loan. One old tried and true trick that just might help a loan officer look at you as a person rather than your three digit credit score is to engage them in conversation about themselves. That's right; find something in their office, if possible, that will tip you off to something about their personal hobbies, interests, family, etc. They might have a bowling or tennis trophy displayed in their office. Maybe they have a picture of their family on a recent ski trip.

You need to be subtle about this form of taking control, but it never hurts to add a personal touch to such an interview by asking, "Oh, wow! I love skiing, and it's obvious you and your family do, too. That looks like Tahoe — is that where it was taken?" With a little practice, you'll become quite expert at this. It serves another purpose, too — it helps you feel less intimidated by the loan officer, and helps you remember that they're simply a person, too. Everyone likes to be asked about themselves, just do it in moderation, so it's not too obvious. When someone realizes you're a nice person who may just have a few things in common with them, they tend to become more open to looking into different avenues through which they might be able to assist you.

So being in control of a conversation, even for a brief period in the grand scheme of things, can help you diffuse tension – often for the other party, as well as yourself. It can also help you come across as more confident, outgoing and as someone who's interested in many things, and in other people, not just yourself. It can also save you a lot of valuable time, when someone else is choosing to hold their own private filibuster which is simply not on topic regarding anything about which you wish to converse.

How to Take Control of a Conversation

In this section we'll look at 22 ways to take control when you're talking to someone. Some of these ideas are simple so we can cover those in a few lines while some require a more detailed explanation and an example. Still, don't overlook the power of a principle just because it is simple. When you stack all the simple ideas, it can dramatically improve your ability to take charge.

Whether you're talking with a family member, significant other/spouse, a friend, a colleague or your boss, there are many advantages to perfecting the art of redirecting, or taking control of a conversation. As the guidelines on how to do this, along with the techniques involved unfold, I will periodically include some case scenario examples to illustrate how you can take control in any given situation and in any conversation.

1. Know your goal for the conversation
Whenever possible, prior to having the conversation, make sure that the right people will be included (i.e., decision-makers, the one(s) you wish to influence, impress, etc.). Keep the meeting open only to those who fit into this category, as others might create distraction. Granted, many conversations start spontaneously, and you may not have a firm objective or outcome in mind at the beginning of one of those. But it's still possible to take control. Here's an example:

Example of a Spontaneous Conversation with Your Significant Other

As soon as you get home from work, your "S.O." starts the conversation with, "Honey, I really want to go out for Chinese food tonight. I'm really craving Chow Fun's food."

You just had Chinese food at Chow Fun's for lunch, so you're not exactly wild about this idea. Still, you like to compromise and keep everyone happy, so you make the following suggestion,

"Yes, Chow Fun's has great food. So great in fact, I ate lunch there today with my boss. Now, I'm willing to go there again for dinner if your heart's really set on it, but what do you think about this? Let's jump online real quickly and read some reviews of that new Thai/Mexican/Italian (your choice) restaurant that you've been wanting to try out – you know, the one that recently opened nearby? If that sounds like something different and interesting, we could give that a try. What do you think?"

This way you have offered to go somewhere you know your S.O. has wanted to check out, but have also successfully extricated yourself from having an overdose of Chow Fun! Simply by suggesting an alternative you took control of the conversation.

Now, let's contrast that with a conversation with your teenaged son that you've been planning for a while.

Example of Pre-planned Conversation with Your Teenaged Son

Your teenaged son Charlie flops down on the sofa and starts to play one of his many video games. You've tried several times to talk to Charlie about the messy condition he leaves the family car in, after taking it out for a drive with his friends.

You start, "Charlie, would you please turn that game off for a while? We need to discuss the car and how you've been treating it, son."

Charlie sighs, and merely pauses his game. You give him a look, and if he doesn't turn it completely off, you take the controller and do it yourself. It's important to make sure you have his full attention since your previous attempts to convey this message haven't gotten through.

"What is it, Dad?"

"Well, you know I've mentioned how annoying it is to get in the car and find it filled with burger wrappers and other trash..."

"Yeah... but, Dad! The guys think I'm really cool when I take them out to grab some food. And we like to eat while we're cruising around."

"Be that as it may, Charlie, here's the deal. I'm really not trying to impinge on your coolness, but from now on, you guys just need to eat at the restaurant, or go to a park. And make sure you always pick up after yourselves there, as well as not leaving any trash at all in the car. I'm talking even a gum wrapper, okay? When you have your own car someday, if you want to keep it like a pigpen, then that's your business. I pity any girlfriends you have, though. For now, the family car means that it needs to be kept clean and neat so that all the family members can use it, any time we need and want, and it should always be left in clean condition for the next user."

"But I don't always have time... ."

"Then you must find the time, son. You're not the only one with a busy schedule, you know. Or maybe next time you want to use the car, I won't have the time or desire to toss you the keys. Now, I need you to go out and clean the car out thoroughly, take it to the car wash, vacuum the insides and wash the outside – bring it back sparkling like new, and smelling good. Otherwise you'll have to ride the bus for your date with Rachel this weekend. Are we clear?"

Charlie gets up with a grunt, but grins at you as you toss him the keys and he heads out the door. You know he really likes Rachel, and you have masterfully used that leverage.

2. Assume a powerful physical presence, i.e. you could stand up for emphasis at some point.

This is particularly effective if you're meeting with someone who wants something from you. Sitting on a chair that's slightly higher than the one they'll be sitting on is an old "trick of kings." You're not going to be on a throne, of course, but just a slight height advantage (3 or 4 inches taller) can make a big impression.

It's also a good way to redirect focus to stand up as a way of indicating the conversation is concluded, or to get up and move a few steps, as though you're deep in thought (and you well may be, strategizing your next point!)

When you're on your "home turf" and really need/want to terminate the conversation, for example, when you're meeting with someone who doesn't know when to conclude the small talk and move on, just do the following, smiling politely the entire time:

Stand up, and sincerely smiling (remember?), cross to the door and open it, maintaining eye contact and continuing to smile, genuinely. Say something to the effect of, "This has been great. Thanks so much for carving time out of your schedule to meet with me. I have another appointment in just a few minutes, but we'll be in touch/I appreciate your time... ." (Whatever best suits the occasion).

Standing up generally takes the other party by surprise, especially if they're still talking! But it's a nonverbal way of getting your point across that you need to get on with your day, whereas trying to tell them in words may not have done the trick!

3. Use an authoritative but pleasant voice; speak from a place of power and calm. This doesn't mean to lull them into a state of submission! Exude enthusiasm while coming across as the expert on – well, the things about which you are an expert. Smiling frequently while discoursing and using humor when it fits easily keeps others at ease and more likely to follow what you're saying, rather than leaning toward "lecturing," which tends to promote loss of interest quickly.

4. Eliminate all distractions; when you choose the meeting point, you are more in control of the environment of the conversation. So whenever possible, grab the opportunity to choose the venue, particularly for very important conversations. Using a little aforethought not only for your own point-making ability, but also to show the other person(s) you care enough to pick a quiet place where you can hear them clearly, as well.

5. Ask questions, to engage interaction and establish you as the "alpha" person. When you're asking questions, you're creating rapport, an interactive exchange, rather than pushing for a "filibuster." Remember, if you keep the conversation more casual and friendly than formal and dictatorial, you'll be more successful in keeping control. It reminds me of a very old saying, "You catch more flies with honey than with vinegar."

6. The Power of Surrender
Sometimes, there is an amazing amount of power that can be achieved by the simple act of surrender. What I mean by this is relaxing and detaching from any attachment to the outcome of the conversation. Now, this does not mean that you are completely giving up on your objective – far from it! But when you remain flexible as to how you go about attaining your desired outcome, in other words, when you "go with the flow," oftentimes you can more readily turn the conversation back in the direction

you wish it to go. If you relax rather than trying to force a point, you will come across as amiable and a good listener; it's when you insist on pushing a point even when the point in the conversation is less than ideal, that you will be perceived as desperate and manipulative. Not your goal, by the way! Subtly yet powerfully taking control is a true art form unto itself.

7. Get agreement, starting with the smaller issues and work your way up.

Pretty self-explanatory. Once you've got the other party agreeing with you on smaller points, they'll be more likely to go the same route on your most important issues. Here's an example:

Example of a Conversation with a Dominant Community/Group Leader

You: "Sally, that's a great point you have there. But wouldn't you agree that when we were writing the bylaws, they came out much more well-stated and stronger when we took those surveys and the community members' suggestions into consideration?"

Sally, "Well, yes, that's right."

You: "Absolutely, I think so, too! And while you have an excellent point here about this new amendment to our Rules of Conduct, don't you think it might be better received if we basically did the same thing now? To incorporate the gist of some of the Board of Directors' suggestions into that amendment?"

Sally, "Yes, I suppose so."

Using a previous example of a past success is often a great way to turn a conversation back in the direction you wish it to take.

8. Establish rapport; set the pace and lead in the direction you wish it to go. In other words, once you've gotten some agreement, engaged interactivity and rapport, then take charge of the flow/pace of the conversation as you skillfully maneuver it in the direction of your choice by mentioning topics you want to discuss and by asking questions to engage others.

9. Periodically respectfully touch the other person's arm; not too much, simply for emphasis on specific points. Many studies have shown that gently touching a person's arm or shoulder in moderation/once in a while opens them up to responding positively to you. NLP practitioners are among the conversation control "masters" who know the power of using light physical contact to get certain points across. Studies have also shown that people who work in industries where they rely upon tips – i.e., waiters, cab drivers, etc., who respectfully (and just once or twice at most) touch a customer's arm or shoulder often get the best tips!

10. Know your specific intended outcome; stay focused upon it, but stay flexible. Once again, you come across as more likeable and easy to talk to/work with, when you're not rigid and/or stubborn about making your point. Keep it lighthearted when the conversation swerves in a different direction; flexibility and humor will go a long way towards getting others to get back on track when the timing is better, further into the conversation.

11. Casually use provocative examples or questions, to elicit objections, and then overcome them. For instance, if you were a fishing lure salesperson:

You: "I was talking with someone just the other day who had great success while using this particular fishing lure on his recent trip to Alaska. He caught more sockeye than ever, he told me. Do you want to know his secret?"

Potential Customer: "Sure, what was it?"

You: "Ever go fishing in Alaska yourself?"

Customer: "Yeah, it's one of my favorite spots!"

You: "Great! Well, here's how he told me he used it... "

Then go into detail. If the customer had not shown interest in Alaska or the salmon there, redirect it to get him/her to talk about their favorite fishing holes, and their favorite type of fish to go after. Then adjust your story accordingly.

12. Draw out the other person(s) goals/intentions for the conversation by asking them directly. This shows that you're not just an interesting person, but also an interested one. When you appeal to someone's ego by making sure their goals are known, in addition to your own, they are more likely to come over to your way of thinking on the points that matter most to you. Do your best to seek solutions during the course of the conversation which create win-wins, so everyone is happy!

13. Tie mutual goals into your suggestions. When you've established the other person's goals by drawing them out (as cited just above), point out how parallel their goals and yours are, and how your suggestions can benefit you both.

14. Ask for what you want, either directly or indirectly. If you don't ask, you can't receive. Period. So get over any shyness about asking, no matter what it's for – a promotion, a contract negotiation point, a loan at the bank. Rehearse asking in the mirror – record yourself rehearsing, and then later, listen and see if you sound relaxed and confident as you ask. It's best to record the rehearsal, and then go do something else for at least an hour. This will keep your listening more objective and honest. It's also good to practice with a family member or friend who will seriously do some role playing with you, and give you honest feedback about your finesse when it comes to asking for what you want.

15. Redirect any wandering off-topic. Here are a couple of examples of how you can do this redirecting:

Example 1 – Sales Pitch
You: "Don't you agree, Mary, that this auto policy suits your needs the best?"
Mary, looking at her watch, "Well, I really need to go now – I'm going to be late for another appointment if I don't. I need some more time to think about it."
You: "I can appreciate having a busy schedule, Mary, and the last thing I want to do is make you late. What if I highlight these main points in an email, then I can call you tomorrow and answer any questions you might have? What time would work best for you?"
This shows respect for their schedule (whether real or a stall technique), but you do not simply give up and let her go – set a definite time to finish the conversation/sales pitch, and use the extra time to really emphasize any personal points about Mary and her needs that you've learned from the first conversation.

Example 2 – Family Meeting

You: (showing a brochure of a potential family reunion venue) "And look how the rooms are all on the first floor, so we can all get around the retreat center quickly, and Grandma and Grandpa have easy access everywhere."

Your pushy cousin Mavis: "I remember last year when Grandpa fell and broke his hip... .do you remember that? I think he was visiting Alice in Sedona... ."

You: "Yes, I do recall that, and I'm so glad his hip healed so nicely. He gets along great now, doesn't he? And since there are no stairs at this retreat center, there's no reason Grandpa and everyone else can't get to all the events easy as 1, 2, 3. Let's take a family vote, shall we?"

16. Utilize small movements/motions to progress your aims. If you resort to using large gestures, you'll come across as overbearing, or possibly too comedic – not taking the conversation seriously enough. But a little gesture or motion for emphasis can be very effective. For instance, tapping on a point on a map when planning a vacation, and then tracing with your finger the route you'll take (this is the route you prefer, naturally), and the sightseeing available along the way.

17. Use T.O.T.E. – Test, Operate, Test, Exit

While this is based on a behavioral model paradigm, it works really well in controlling a conversation as well. This model encourages you to take a trial and error approach to conversation, keep trying different ideas until you find what works best. Here is an example:

Test: "Do you like these flowers for the wedding?"
"No."
Operate: (Walking toward another flower arrangement)
Test: "What about these? They match Sherry's colors for the wedding, right?" "Yes, those are perfect!"
Exit – Order the flowers that match the wedding colors.

When using comparisons in the course of a conversation, the T.O.T.E. model may require a few more Test/Operates before finally arriving at the Test that is the agreed upon objective, leading to the Exit (successful finish of the conversation)

18. K.I.S.S. – Keep it Simple, Sovereign

Make your main point(s) and don't elaborate too much; schedule future conversations if need be, to cover other topics/situations. You may be an amazing multi-tasker, but not everyone is, and some people tend to get overwhelmed or confused if you present too much in one fell swoop. So scheduling successive (or if need be, step by step) follow-up meetings may be your best solution. The more you train yourself to observe people's responses during conversation, their nervous habits (looking at their watch, drumming the table, humming to themselves, etc.) you'll get to be a star "detective" at figuring out their ideal limit when it comes to attention span and how much to present in each sound-bite meeting.

19. **Only answer what you want**; ignore any silly remarks.

If you find yourself engaged in a conversation with a smart a... .well, I'll be nice and say "smart aleck," don't allow yourself to be suckered into answering questions you're uncomfortable with, or that detract from your main objective. Redirect the conversation by changing the subject, or by using the old technique of answering a question with a question, to redirect it. And if your fellow conversationalist is really good at throwing the bull around, you don't need to get out your shovel – just be the bigger person and ignore their silliness, and refocus the conversation's energy where you need and want it to go.

20. **Stay cool, calm & collected**

if the other party tries to rock your emotional state in order to gain control. They might be a master at buffaloing you with silly comments. (as mentioned above) or really know how to push all of your buttons (this is especially true of relatives and significant others) Remember, you are the one in control of your emotions and how long you choose to experience them – nobody is holding a gun to your head and telling you how to feel, after all. Or if they are, you need to control more than just a conversation! Seriously, though, take a few nice, deep, centered breaths anytime you feel yourself sliding down a slippery emotional slope and release any negative feelings. Then turn your valued attention back to what's important in the moment – reaching your goal!

21. Practice slow, deep diaphragmatic breathing before and during the conversation to keep yourself thinking clearly; this helps with staying calm and levelheaded. Basically just a fleshed-out extension of the advice above. But deep breathing is good to practice throughout the conversation. The more oxygenation you send to your lungs and as a result your bloodstream, the more oxygen will flow to your brain, keeping you focused and calm. It's much easier to take control of a conversation from this standpoint than from one of panic and anxiety. B R E A T H E!

22. Carefully listen and watch for any unspoken issues/hidden agendas, and don't hesitate to ask for clarity, right then and there. Everyone has a "tell" – what tips someone's hand when they're bluffing in cards. But the more diligent practice you put into mastering the control of a conversation, the more you'll learn people's "tells" when they are uncomfortable with something you're proposing, or have a secondary agenda with regard to a certain point they are pushing just a bit too hard. Go ahead! Scratch the surface, and ask, "If that scenario you've brought up a few times were to come about, what would be the main advantage for you?" They may be flattered, or possibly offended; hopefully either way, you'll get an answer.

It's better to be direct than to waste everyone's time and energy beating around the bush. A way to "see" someone's resistance is through body language, of course. When someone is crossing their arms across their chest, that's a sure sign they're not open to what you're proposing, or that they're protecting themselves from something they don't want to hear, or perhaps don't understand. Shift gears, get them to relax and smile, interject some humor about something totally off-topic for just a few seconds to shift the mood, then bring it back where you want the conversation to head.

Ways People Lose Control of a Conversation

In this section we'll look at 15 common ways people lose control of a conversation. We need to be aware of these common mistakes and stop making them. We also need to look out for them when others are talking because those mistakes on their part represent opportunities for us to step in and take back control!

1. When someone feels nervous, antsy and/or intimidated right off the bat, they tend to just roll over and relinquish control, thereby giving it to others and allowing them to lead the direction of the conversation.

2. Failure to listen, therefore ignoring key signals from others. Developing your skills as a good listener, as well as a careful observer of body language, will go far in helping you maintain or regain control of a conversation. But if you're so intent on your own objective that you're not really listening to the other party and what they want, it will become painfully obvious to them right away, and more than likely, the conversation will come to a grinding halt, without you getting even one step closer to achieving your objective. So don't forget there has to be a give and take, much like a game of tennis or ping-pong – you must listen, watch and respond appropriately, not just continuing to smash the ball in a way that doesn't allow the other person to return your serve, so to speak. So "keep your ears on" and your radar attuned to what the other person/people are seeking, as well as your own goals.

3. Annoying others by ignoring their outcome and/or values. This pretty much goes hand in hand with not listening, described above. When you ignore someone's desired outcome, or run roughshod over their value system, they'll find you a rude bore. Now when was the last time you enjoyed talking with a rude bore? Pay attention – LISTEN and respond appropriately. Smile and engage the participation of everyone involved.

4. Fixating on a minor issue and losing sight of the primary goal. This is akin to the old saying that goes, "You can't see the forest for the trees." Don't let one "tree" that might crop up unexpectedly deter you from your most important objective. If it's something that will make the other party more agreeable overall to what you desire, be flexible – negotiate!

5. Answering questions too quickly due to nerves; failure to think through giving an answer that will allow you to maintain control. Many people rush to give an answer without ruminating upon it for a few moments, or even a minute or two. Never over-promise and under-deliver, if the question has to do with what you're able or willing to do. If it requires that you do some research prior to giving an informed answer, just be honest and tell them you need some time to come up with the fairest answer for all concerned. Be sure you write down the point, or are making an audio note/record of it, so they know you're serious, and so you remember to follow through! Once you've taken enough time to think it through, whether in that particular conversation, or a bit further down the road, then you can simply redirect the conversation towards your goal and move forward.

6. Letting fear of failure prevent you from going for what you want. Remember the old mnemonic device – "Fear is False Evidence Appearing Real?" It's quite true. Usually we become afraid of something before it's even occurred, or without having all of the details. Focus on your solution, your goal, rather than on your fear of failure. Going into a conversation knowing what you want and having the confidence to get your point(s) across will help you reach that objective; fear is a "freezer" – it prevents you from moving forward, keeps you stuck, and often causes people to mumble or just give up far too easily. Be brave, bold and eloquent, while staying respectful of the other party's goals, too. You never know until you try, so go for it! Or as a best seller book title proclaimed years ago, "Feel the Fear and Do It Anyway!"

7. Failure to build a series of small wins before seeking your major outcome/goal(s). It's SO important to cultivate agreement via a series of "baby steps," if you will, prior to diving right in and going after your major goals like a dog with a bone. If you're too aggressive about your primary objective and don't give rapport some time to build and strengthen, you'll come across as desperate, pushy or both. Not the way to convince someone to align with you! Take your time, use some questions to get those "yeses" accumulating, and once the other person is already in the mindset of saying "yes" – then that is the time to go for your big target, but smoothly, and calmly, remember. When you get really good at this, they may not even be aware which one of your goals was your main point! They will just know they like and admire your style, and agree with you.

8. Allowing others to drive/trigger your emotional state. This is a really big one, particularly with relatives, close friends or colleagues. When people know you really well and have an innate knowledge of how to "go for your emotional jugular," well, that's just someplace you don't want to go. You'll lose every time, if you allow this to happen. Remember – nobody is forcing you to feel a particular way; they're not holding a gun to your head telling you how to feel, right? You're in charge of that, no one else.

9. And since forewarned is forearmed, if you're about to engage in a conversation with someone who you know from past experience has pushed all your buttons, simply make sure you take plenty of time to relax and center before your meeting. You might even like to imagine a shield or a suit of armor woven of translucent white light that only you can see, protecting you from any type of attack or provocation. It's often especially effective to make sure you have lots of this white light protection around the center of your chest (the "heart chakra" area) as well as your solar plexus – where those "gut reactions" kick in. Imagine the light deflecting any attempted digs or trigger pushes.

10. Another great phrase to bear in mind prior to engaging in such conversations is, "What you think of me is none of my business." Know who you are, know thyself, in other words. And don't worry about what the other person may think of you, or how they may have been successful manipulating you in the past. You're more savvy now, you've taken time to prepare and be on the defensive (quietly, without confrontation). Using humor to redirect a conversation is always another great way to deflect negative feelings and prevent you from getting emotionally unbalanced.

11. Simply giving up when roadblocks appear, rather than focusing on win-wins, and allowing the perceived problem/challenge to grow. It's sad but true that a large part of human nature involves unconditional surrender far too early. Giving up when a problem seems insurmountable, rather than (mentally) taking a giant step back in order to see the big picture, and focusing on co-creating solutions and win-wins. Sometimes it's actually good to acknowledge that a potential problem has been brought up in advance:

"Joe, I'm really glad you brought that concern to the forefront. Why don't we do a bit of brainstorming about how we might overcome that, should it arise?"

That way, you are fostering a team spirit, rather than having a defeatist attitude and throwing in the towel. Sometimes facing the worst possible case scenario in advance helps you come up with well thought-out solutions in the event that problem ever should rear its ugly head. Then you simply put your solution-based plan into action. Simple!

12. Allowing your ego to push you into losing a key point or outcome. Too often, people let their competitive nature (i.e., ego) force them into "pushing beyond the point of no return" when it feels like they have relinquished control of a conversation, or haven't yet achieved their goal. So if you notice any temptation to allow "snarkiness" or sarcasm to insidiously come creeping into your side of the talk, it's really a good idea to hold your tongue, take some deep breaths, smile and see if there's a creative way to bring the conversation back around your way. If the other party has viewpoints which you don't share, live and let live; agree to disagree, but don't become combative or confrontational.

Smooth, suave and in control is the key. And even if you don't "win" this particular conversation, at least you won't have burned any bridges, and the other party will still think you're a nice person. Better that than to remove all doubt from their mind that you're an egomaniac! That only works for dictators, you know – and look what usually winds up happening to most of them!

13. Boring others with too much personal detail; this incites them to stop listening and ultimately, from making a committed agreement. Even if you have a great example story that you feel will help your point come across, perhaps a smarter way to present it would be the old, "You know, a friend of mine had great success when they tried something similar... ." and then go ahead with the story.

14. As far as just giving way too much TMI about yourself, limit what you share to the context of the conversation, or what you're comfortable answering, when asked any type of personal question. Keeping a slight air of mystery can sometimes be prudent; and let's face it, unless you're a celebrity, most people don't really want to know all the gory (or tedious) details of your life. Focus on what you're aiming to achieve and don't waste anyone's time with unnecessary details.

15. Allowing a fast talker to keep you from getting a word in edgewise. You know, some people are just naturally fast, nonstop talkers. Perhaps this stems from their own nervousness, or in some cases, loneliness (i.e., you might be the only person who's listened to them for a long time). Or maybe they just have "narcissus ears" and simply are in love with the sound of their own voice. Whatever the case may be, since you're engaged in conversation with them and obviously have a desired outcome in mind, if you allow them to run on without allowing you to bring up your own agenda in any way, shape or form, then you've lost before you've begun. Because you haven't made sure they let you begin. Here are some ways to get Chatty Cathy to pause for breath and listen to you:

Chatty Cathy: "And then we went to the cutest little store where we found the most adorable little stuffed animal pillows, and oh! That reminds me, my dog Zsa Zsa did the most outrageous thing the other day... .yada, yada, yada... ."

You (politely interjecting): "Oh, you have a dog named Zsa Zsa? What breed is she?"

Chatty Cathy: (Possibly startled that someone has actually been paying much attention to what she's been prattling on about) Oh, yes! Zsa Zsa is my toy poodle. She's the love of my life!"

You: "Dogs are great, aren't they? And that's part of why I wanted to talk with you about this particular location for our cappuccino cart, down on the corner of Main and 3rd, you know? Because there are so many dog lovers who walk their pooches around that area – we could give away free doggie treats and have some water bowls there, so it's not all just about the people. Don't you agree that location is the ideal place for us to set up shop?"

Just one example. Bear in mind that a very effective way to get the "Cathys" in your life to listen to what you have to say is to acknowledge something about their endless stream of words, then get their agreement on a common issue. After that, it's much easier to keep their rapt attention (at least for a while, as a rule), and focus upon what you're really meeting to talk about in the first place.

Again, it often comes down to showing the other person that you truly are a nice, considerate person. Don't you prefer to do business, or make plans (whether business or personal) with someone who's nice? And as tempting as it might be to just interrupt their tirade at times and scream, "Don't you ever take a breath or shut up, for gosh sakes?" – that's never going to win you any brownie points, as they say, and certainly not going to further your cause or goal. So again, exercise patience, breathe deeply, but when that perfect place to jump in and create actual two-way communication presents itself, then butting in is not perceived as impolite, but interested. There's a huge difference, isn't there? And wouldn't you agree that getting someone to agree with you is easier if you ask a question once in awhile? You get the picture.

How to Regain Self-Control When Someone Disturbs You

Some scenarios have already been covered about ways to regain control, but this next section is more about things you can do inwardly, to help yourself feel grounded and centered again before you get back in the game with the conversation. One really great thing about these techniques is, nobody but you will know you're doing them – they're that subtle! But don't underestimate their value – they can be quite empowering, just when you need it most.

1. Breathing
The value of taking nice, long, slow diaphragmatic breaths has been discussed a bit, but since "repetition is the mother of skill," it never hurts to touch upon good information again; possibly to revisit it in a slightly different way, or with a bit more detail thrown in for emphasis.

When a baby is first born (including you!) they automatically breathe deeply and fully, from the diaphragm muscle. If you doubt this at all, just observe a little baby breathing while it sleeps – its tummy will gently rise and fall with its breath. So where did we go astray and begin doing more shallow breathing? For most of us, pretty much when we started walking and running – suddenly that need to get places quickly and do things as fast as possible (part of the learning intake process behavior of toddlers) kicks into overdrive, and poof! That autonomic breathing seldom happens, at least not while in the awake state. Runners, swimmers, yoga practitioners, students of meditation, and singers learn, or better stated -relearn – the importance of exercising the diaphragm and breathing deeply to create more energy, more stamina, and in the case of singers, more volume and projection. But if, like the majority of people, you haven't ever really had the need or opportunity to relearn and practice the art of deep breathing, then it's time!

Not only will taking those long, slow deep breaths calm your nerves and balance your heart rate, it will also clear your mind as more oxygen travels throughout your bloodstream, and gets to your brain. The "brain fog" that many modern day multi-taskers suffer from could well become a thing of their past if they were conscientiously begin to practice deep, diaphragmatic breathing.

Practice it on a frequent basis; it's good for you! After all, it's the way we came into this physical world, breathing deeply and naturally. It's the way our bodies were designed to function. It's just that in the Western "civilized" world (that can be an oxymoron, but never mind for now), we often get into such a big hurry to receive instant gratification for just about everything, we forget how to properly do something that is more essential to our existence than eating and drinking – breathing. You can go for days without food, and for quite a while without water, but not for more than a few seconds without breath. Ponder that for a bit, and start practicing deep breathing regularly. You'll notice that by breathing deeply while driving, you have more patience with other drivers' behavior, and you're also more clear-headed so you can more readily drive defensively – your awareness is sharpened. This is true with many other behaviors as well.

With regard to the importance of deep breathing during a conversation, having built up your stamina and breath support allows to you express yourself easily and eloquently without searching for breath. Seriously. And if you're a bit overweight, using that diaphragm is also a good way to exercise your waistline area. When you inhale, you should feel your waistline expand. Singers and others are taught this simple trick to make sure they're breathing deeply and fully:

Place your hands on your waistline – actually, so that the tips of your middle fingers are lightly touching, just above your navel. When you inhale, filling up the diaphragm, the tips of those fingers will be pushed slightly apart as your waistline expands. Then as you exhale, strive to keep that expansion for as long as you can without running out of breath. That's the exercise part! If you really want to develop that power even more, you can get a three to five pound sandbag and while lying flat on the ground or the floor (or upon a yoga mat would actually be more sanitary), then place the sandbag in the same position, right around the navel, and breathe in and out, causing the sandbag to gently rise and fall with each deep, rhythmic breath. It's a good way to actually see and feel that you're breathing properly.

So here's another part of the beauty of all of this – breathing deeply, especially once you've become accustomed to doing it regularly – is something that no one else will pick up on, or be able to detect that you're doing in order to stay calm and laser focused.

Let's take this one step further, shall we? Let's say you've been talking to your Uncle Larry, who has always had a habit of being able to "get your goat," or cause a knee-jerk emotional reaction out of you by pushing your infamous buttons. Well, next time you're around an "Uncle Larry" type, here's another tool you can employ which will go completely undetected, but it will help you tremendously:

As you're taking those nice, slow deep breaths, very slowly and gently, bring your fingertips in to touch the center of your palms, making a very loose, relaxed fist. Do this as you inhale – and hold that breath for just a few moments. Notice where you feel any tension in your body, and decide that as you exhale, you're going to release that tension, as well as any negativity "Larry" may have aimed in your direction. As you exhale, relax your fingertips and point them toward the floor, imagining that all of that tension, negativity, and really anything else that is not serving your Highest Good is simply draining right out of your fingers and into the floor or the ground. Now, if you're one of those people who is worried about harming the earth or the environment by releasing such negative energy, then just do so with the intention that Mother Earth has the ability to shift and transform it into something that will behoove and serve Her – maybe along the lines of transmuting it and using it to help her stabilize Her core.

This may sound all "airy-faerie" to some of you, but to others who are all too aware that thoughts are things and that we are all made up of energy (quantum physicists are masters of this knowledge and power), it will make sense. Regardless, you'll find that using the finger-flex technique with the deep breathing will help you feel centered quickly and easily, and no one else will be the wiser. It might also help to think to yourself as you exhale, "Cancel, Cancel" or "Erase, Erase," "Delete, Delete," – whatever word you choose to help your subconscious mind work with you in releasing something that is not serving your best interests. Then on the next inhalation, think of something that makes you smile, or for which you're grateful. It's not just the Universe that abhors a vacuum – your subconscious mind does, too! But when you let something go, unless you fill that "void" with something else that's positive, the negative feeling or thought will creep back in, pretty rapidly. That's simply the way our brains are wired. Put this exercise to the test, and I'm willing to wager you'll find it helps you with many situations; particularly with regaining your composure and focus when heading towards regaining control of a conversation!

2. Visualization

Using visualization to create your desired outcome is a tool that should never be underestimated, just like the power of breathing. Here are two easy ways to employ it, with regard to regaining control of a conversation.

1) Balance Your Brain!

There's a strip of neurons which separate/connect your left and right brain hemispheres; that strip is called the corpus callosum. This arched band of nerve fibers allows both sides of your brain to communicate. Most people process life and its experiences more with one side or the other of the brain – i.e., artistic, creative individuals tend to be more right-brained, while scientists, accountants, and other just generally logical, analytically minded folks lean more toward left-brain dominance. You'll be amazed how good this left/right brain balancing technique makes you feel.

Shower Power! Mentally tune into that corpus callosum. As you inhale, imagine it filling up with brilliant white light that is filled with calm wisdom and healing, from Divine Source, if you believe in that, or simply from Universal Energy, if you're more comfortable with that paradigm. Hold the breath for a count of 3, and then as you exhale, silently tell yourself, "Shower, shower, shower," and imagine that beautiful white light flowing equally over both sides of your remarkable brain – still the most amazing computer on earth. Do this 2 or 3 times until you feel yourself calm and rebalanced, and then you'll be more able to smoothly and intelligently find the means of taking control of the conversation again. And as a bonus – once again, no one else has a clue of the course correcting, empowering tool you just used.

But they'll notice you have more energy, a light in your eyes and a sense of calm and strength — always a good place to be when making your point!

2) Visualize it Happening!

Before you make your move to regain control, take a few moments to tune into what it will feel, sound and look like. It's as simple as that. Athletes who visualize successfully completing their event or other sports activities have been hooked up to electrodes which measure their muscle response while they're visualizing, and lo and behold, the same muscle groups fire while they're simply running the event in their mind! So there's scientific evidence that visualization can help create your success. It's another way of rehearsing for your smash hit play called "Life!" Or in this case, "Regaining Control of a Conversation in a Scene from the Play Called Life." Try It — it's free!

How to Prepare in Advance to Ensure Success

Old adages have been around for decades, and in some cases centuries, for good reason. It's because they are often infused with sage wisdom. For instance, are you familiar with the one that goes, "An ounce of prevention is worth a pound of cure"? Well, that applies to the art of controlling a conversation in this way:

When you take the time to prepare in advance for an upcoming scheduled meeting/conversation, you're better equipped to avoid pitfalls, or to know how to handle expected objections, etc. By practicing some of the following tips and techniques, you'll build your confidence level, be perceived as a master of conversation, and more often than not, be able to reach your goals. So let's get started!

1. Create your game plan – clarify your goals before you even set up the conversation.

Basically, make sure you know beyond a shadow of a doubt what your end objective, your best case scenario outcome from the conversation is. Examine both sides of the equation here – in other words, look at how your goal will be mutually beneficial, so you can point out to the other person how conjoint agreement will bring benefit to them – not just to you. This needs to be a sincere benefit, not just so many words, so do some good pre-planning.

2. Visualize/rehearse the meeting in your mind; even go so far as to act it out, possibly even video tape or record it so you have the most accurate picture of how you'll look & sound. The camera doesn't lie, and this is a technique often employed by actors and public speakers so they can actually put themselves in the audience's shoes, or in your case, the other conversationalist's shoes. Stay objective as you watch the playback – if you didn't know the person on camera (you), would you trust them? Why or why not? If there are areas for improvement (trust me, there almost always are), what's required to make those improvements? For example, if it's making better eye contact (no one likes talking to someone with "shifty" eyes, or who is so self-conscious they always look at the ground, never directly at them — then you need to practice making better eye contact. It's that simple. Now, practicing in the mirror or on camera for this is good, but putting it into practical application — superb! And those with whom you're practicing don't even have to know they're helping you. How, you ask?

Simple. Make eye contact, at least more than you've normally been comfortable with, with everyone you can. The cashier at the grocery store; people on the bus or subway; strangers on the street — don't stare, just nod and smile. Not everyone will play along, especially complete strangers, but you'll be surprised — most people will! Sometimes people walking down the street are feeling as lonely or self-conscious as you might be. A friendly smile, eye contact and a nod might just make their day, and it puts you one step closer to building up your own confidence, so don't be shy! Once you become more comfortable with making eye contact, then progress on to a line or two of small talk, particularly if you're good with making humorous remarks. Laughter is very healing, and even a comment made by a witty stranger can help someone have a better day. Practice makes perfect, so seize every opportunity you have to improve in the areas you made note of that need fine-tuning. Chances to practice are out there, available to all of us each and every day. Make use of them, and have fun along the way. It doesn't have to be deadly serious (in fact, it's much better if it's not!)

3. Take time before the meeting to get yourself centered and focused (i.e., allow plenty of time to get ready before-hand, avoid anything/anyone that might cause you to become emotionally out of balance). This is VERY important, especially if the upcoming conversation's goals are really big ones for you — such as asking for a promotion/raise, a loan or investment opportunity, a key turning point in a relationship, etc.

Again, the rehearsing beforehand can prove to be invaluable, so don't discount that. But simply making sure you create the time in advance to prepare and center is extremely important. Also taking every precaution possible to make sure that you have a good night's sleep prior to the meeting is an excellent form of preparedness. By doing that in addition to taking a few minutes just before the meeting, you go into it feeling rested, calm, cool and collected, and focused on your agenda rather than emotionally, physically or mentally exhausted.

4. Take care of your physical needs. Stay hydrated. It's amazing how dry one's mouth and throat can become while talking. Coffee is a diuretic, so if you're meeting at Starbuck's or another coffee place, make sure you have a glass or bottle of water handy, in addition to any java. If your throat has a bit of a tickle, take some cough drops or lozenges with you. Better that you nurse one of those and be able to continue talking than to cough and hack your way through the conversation. If "nature calls" during the meeting, don't be shy about excusing yourself. It's very important that you feel comfortable and relaxed throughout the meeting, and if you ignore your bodily needs, the last thing you're going to come across as, is comfortable. All of this is just good common sense, obviously, but go ahead and put it into practice. It will all work to your advantage, so why not do it?

What Skills Do You Need to Strengthen to Maintain Control?

Okay, it's time to "get real" with yourself; unbridled self-honesty is called for in order to become as effective at controlling a conversation as possible. If you already know what your strengths are from past successes (where you've held or regained control of a conversation), write down those strengths that have worked.

On the opposite side of the coin, if you're aware of your weaknesses, then you need to write those down as well. In fact, those are actually more important to know and understand than your strengths, aren't they? You probably already know a few of those weaknesses — do any of these sound familiar?

- You find yourself feeling short of breath when you feel like you've been put on the spot or when the conversation's control has flipped to the other person
- Your palms get sweaty, and perhaps you're perspiring in other places more than usual as well
- You tend to stammer or feel tongue-tied when the other person assumes control
- You let yourself become easily distracted during the course of the conversation, and then never manage to bring it back around to your true agenda, thereby missing your goal altogether

There may be others, but these are a few common ones. And you know what? We have now covered several tools that with just a bit of diligent practice on your part, can help you balance, correct and overcome ANY of these weaknesses, as well as many other reactions or "spots" you might find yourself in, during a conversation. None of these are life-threatening, so just relax. Practice, practice, practice, remember? It's not just the way to "get to Carnegie Hall" — it is something that's required in any facet of life in order to master a skill — including being an effective communicator and controller of conversations.

One great way to honestly discover both your strengths and weaknesses in conversational art is to simply ask the other party if they mind if you record the conversation. A digital voice recorder is great for this, and many people's phones today have the ability to do so as well. You can just tell them that you plan to transcribe the meeting highlights later (which you do, but for your own self-enlightenment as much as to help you remember what was said). Just like the camera doesn't lie (with the previously suggested videotaping) neither does the audio recording. You may be surprised to hear the inflection in your voice during specific parts of the conversation. This is an amazing self-education tool, so I encourage you to use it regularly. Remember, there's always room for improvement! When we get too cocksure of ourselves about anything, that's when we're often most vulnerable; keep some humility, and be willing to learn from your mistakes, or uncertainties.

So assess, fine-tune, improve and move toward mastery of controlling conversations. It can enhance virtually every area of your life — better physical health, mental clarity, emotional stability, spiritual peace, and even increased financial gain. It depends upon the situation, the conversation, and how you maneuver it to achieve your goals. You're in the driver's seat — so talk with confidence, consideration and the continued willingness to improve this skill — and you'll wind up on the road to success — every time.

Section 2

52 Conversation Blueprints

This section is made up of the 52 conversation blueprints you can use in a variety of situations to take control of the conversation. You do of course have to exercise intelligence and flexibility when applying the tips – developing great conversation skills is an art. With practice, you'll find creative ways to apply what you learn here and make it your own. You'll adapt these new learnings to express more of your personality and to take charge with style!

Although every conversation is unique there are fundamental principles and approaches that offer you a much higher possibility of success. That is what I have focused on in the blueprints.

Okay, with that said, let's get started....

How to Get People to Admire You

To get people to admire you, you need to be someone who is worthy of admiration. You can gain the admiration of those around you by following a recipe. The dish you will have prepared is yourself: a better developed, more admirable you.

So, what do you need to get people to admire you?

First, you need to have developed good character traits. Then you need to mix in some integrity and a good value system to which you adhere. Lastly, you need to add a good dash of social skills to communicate these to other people. All these elements contribute to encouraging people to admire you.

1. Be selfless

Selflessness allows you to make people feel loved and appreciated without you necessarily expecting anything in return. This can be as simple as being a good listener when people need someone to talk to. Giving up some of your time to help other people, in charity work or just to do something good for a family member or friend is an admirable thing to do.

2. Be tolerant

People will be more likely to admire you if you make them feel special. This involves being tolerant of other people's views and actions. Also, if you are tolerant of life's ups and downs you still come up smiling, that is something people will find admirable.

3. Be honest

No one admires a fake, so you need to be honest to gain other people's admiration. That means you must genuinely care about people and demonstrate that to them so they believe it.

Behave genuinely with other people and let them know your real feelings. Even if you have something potentially upsetting to tell people, tell them. Just be sensitive about how you do that.

4. Have integrity

Develop a set of core values by which you live your life and then stick to them so that people know what they can expect from you. Don't do anything for money and don't do anything to the detriment of other people.

5. Be trustworthy

If you say you will do something, do it. Be the person that other people can rely on when they need help or someone to talk to. Keep people's confidences and give good, honest and unbiased advice where it is asked for.

6. Be sensitive and thoughtful

Don't trample on other people's feelings or make them feel stupid for thinking or feeling in a particular way. So, think about how what you do or say will affect other people.

7. Be optimistic

There is already so much negativity in the world. People who are negative appear to be fearful and bitter. That is not admirable. Do, demonstrate that you see the good in anything and people will admire you and follow your example. They will want to be like you.

8. Develop your self confidence

To inspire admiration, you have to look like someone who sticks to their principles and knows what they want out of life. All this takes self confidence to roll with the punches when life knocks you down and to stick with your principles even if other people disagree with you or even criticize you for your views.

Remember, no one is admired by everyone and you will always run the risk of meeting people who will try to damage your self confidence and say that you are living your life the wrong way.

If you have strong self confidence and your behavior lives up to the above criteria you have developed a good strategy to get people to admire you.

How to Get People to Agree With You

The secret to getting people to agree with you lies in how you approach and talk to them. There are some simple techniques you can learn, some based on the psychologically well respected method of neurolinguistic programming.

You can use these techniques to get people to agree with you, whether that is in negotiating a pay rise, selling your house or in any other situation where you need to get people on your side.

1. Anchoring

This neurolinguistic programming method is about laying the groundwork for getting people to agree with you. First, ask the person you want to agree with you a few closed questions that require a yes or no answer. Make sure you include some questions where they need to answer no, too.

When they give you a 'yes' answer, reward them with a warm smile. Also, make some kind of subtle gesture; it doesn't matter what the gesture is; it can be something as simple as touching your chin with your finger. Alternatively, when you get a 'no' answer, do not smile; retain a serious look and give a different gesture which cannot be mistaken for the other gesture you give for 'yes' answers.

This will have anchored the positive and negative responses in your audience's mind. Now you are ready to ask the important question to which you want a 'yes' answer. As you ask, use the gesture you used for 'yes' answers. This should have resonance in the subconscious mind of the person you are asking and they should be preprogrammed to say 'yes'.

2. Presuppositions

These are a very powerful aspect of neurolinguistic programming. Presuppositions involve you presupposing what an outcome will be as if it was inevitable. Phrases like 'before we sign on the deal, would you care for a drink?' are really useful. It presents a choice, although the two aspects of the apparent choice are not in any way linked. You are steering them in the right direction for what you want.

Of course, you will need to make the supposition of the contract being signed more than once in the conversation. But once you have done this a few times, so long as you don't scare the other person off by being too blatant, their subconscious mind will accept that they have reached that conclusion you seek. It will seem like it is what you both wanted all along.

There are a few different presuppositions that you can use:

3. Alternatives

"Do you want to go for a drink or for dinner on Saturday" presupposes that you will indeed be going out on Saturday, as you wanted to.

4. Numeric Indicators

"Do you want to go to the gallery first or to the studio?" presupposes that you will be going to both places without sounding too pushy.

5. Timed suppositions

Here, words such as 'now', 'after' and 'then' are used. So, you could say: "Would you like me to give you my number now or when we leave?" Either way, they're getting your number!

Time can be twisted too, so that your presuppositions are more subtle when you they need them to be. So, for instance, you could ask, "Should we finish our drinks here or out on the balcony?" That shows the presupposition that the other person will want to remain in your company.

These are a few simple neurolinguistic programming techniques you can familiarize yourself with to get people to agree with you. Just make sure to only use these techniques with integrity to ensure it's a win win for everyone concerned.

Presuppositions are powerful tools that can be used with subtlety to agree easily with someone. They are particularly effective if you have set the scene with some anchoring, too.

How to Get People to Answer Your Questions

Sometimes, all you want are answers. You might feel that your questions are simple, but still find it very difficult to get a straight answer that you can understand. Although that may be a sign of bad communication by those answering you, it could also be that you are not asking in the right way.

Here then are a few tips to get people to answer your questions:

1. Ask several people

This works in many ways. First, if you require a piece of information, it could be that the person you ask first genuinely doesn't know the answer. Also, however, sometimes even if you just want an opinion, it is better to get this from several people. That way, you get an idea of the consensus view.

By using email or instant messenger you should have no trouble asking your questions of several people at one time or at least very quickly.

2. State a wrong answer

Sometimes people who won't willingly stick their neck out and give you what they think is an answer will have no problem with setting you straight if they think you've got it wrong!

This method works particularly well (perhaps unfortunately) in an email that is addressed to several people, as human nature makes people want to show off and be the first to show everyone they know the answer. Don't be worried about that. No one can know everything and not knowing this particular point should not be taken as a sign of weakness in you at all.

3. Ask important questions

If you want a proper, sensible answer from people, don't insult their intelligence or waste their time with useless questions. If you can easily find out an answer by doing some research yourself, do that, rather than asking other people.

That way, you know that the questions you ask other people are genuine and worthwhile. Ask questions which get right to the heart of what you want to know. That will also motivate people to help you out with the answers.

4. Be specific with your questions

This will help people to answer your questions with the correct information. Also, if people don't understand your question they may be deterred from trying to answer you at all. There's nothing in it for them by asking you to clarify yourself and they won't want to look foolish by answering the wrong question so they won't bother to answer you at all.

5. Ask the right person

First you should make sure you find out everything you can about the issue that puzzles you. By gathering knowledge, you can pick away at what you don't understand and arrive at a very specific question. Then it's time to look for an expert or at least someone with personal experience, to answer your specific question.

6. Learn from the answers

People love to be asked questions, because it compliments them. It suggests you respect them and see them as a knowledgeable person. However, no one wants to be referred to often as if they were a perpetual source of all knowledge. They also don't want to see that you did nothing about the answers they gave you.

Therefore, you should make a record of any answers if you are likely to forget them. Then act on the answers. Of course, you may disagree with some answers you get, so of course you won't implement those, but you should at least be prepared to defend your decision regarding this, if you are asked by the person that advised you. And do it politely. Show that you respected their answer but felt it was not quite right for you.

By following these points you can ask good questions, get useful answers, and make the other person feel good and positive about the communication with you, so they will be willing to answer more of your questions when and if they arise in thefuture.

How to Get People to Appreciate You

There is nothing worse than feeling that other people don't appreciate the efforts that you make at work or the favors that you do for your friends and family. It makes you feel unvalued.

Here are some ways you can get people to appreciate you more at work.

1. Learn to appreciate yourself

The way you regard yourself will usually set the standard for how other people see you. Start by recognizing your own good qualities, and be aware of your worth. This will help you to build up your confidence and self esteem, which will make people sit up and notice you more.

If you perceive any weaknesses in yourself try to work on overcoming them. If necessary, take some night classes or ask your supervisor if you can undertake staff training to improve your skills.

2. Don't alienate your boss and colleagues with your attitude

Don't be negative as this creates a bad atmosphere and will certainly put people off you. Even if other people are moaning and complaining try not to get sucked into it. You never know if something negative you say will get back to your manager.

Don't join in with office gossip either.

3. Don't delay people too much when they are trying to get on with their work

We all need help and advice sometimes, but you will certainly not be appreciated if you can't do anything on your own initiative. If you do have a serious problem with your work go straight to your supervisor or manager and ask for their assistance.

Believe it or not your boss will appreciate this more than if you did something wrong and wasted the company's time and money.

4. Show your supervisor or manager that you are reliable and hardworking

Always arrive at work on time and don't take unauthorized days off. Don't sneak off to the restroom or slip out of work early because you've got a date.

Be willing to work a little overtime if you are asked as this will make a good impression.

5. You can add to this good impression by being well organized

Each day make a list of all the tasks you have to do and then prioritize them. You may need to be flexible if other more urgent jobs crop up during the day but at least nothing will be forgotten.

If you want your boss to appreciate you make sure you always submit your work on schedule and that it is of a satisfactory standard.

6. Sometimes, let someone else take the credit for your ideas or work

We all know that you are the one who really deserves the merit, but if you let your supervisor or line manager get the credit for a job well done they will appreciate you all the more for it.

7. Help out your colleagues when they need support

To get your work colleagues to appreciate you you should always be willing to help out even if it means giving up your lunch break.

Try to become a good listener when your workmates have problems and never betray their confidence.

8. Encourage the other people that you work with and praise their efforts

Remember they want to be appreciated just as much as you do and by making them feel better about themselves they will also feel better about you.

9. Work on getting your company's clients to appreciate you

You can do this by being helpful, polite and giving them a high standard of service. Often, you will find that the client will praise you to your supervisor or line manager if you have been particularly helpful, and that will earn your boss' appreciation for improving the public image of the company.

10. Make yourself indispensable

Make sure that you always have all the information about your current project to hand, get to know all the company's regular clients, and always keep your eyes open for opportunities to make the company more efficient or more economical.

To sum up, if you want to get people to appreciate you at work, be organized, efficient, courteous and helpful. Don't just put in the minimum amount of effort to get the job done but go the extra mile and give your company added value.

How to Get People to Be Nice to You

The secret to getting people to be nice to you is to look objectively at the way you behave with other people. You can't control other people's behavior, making them be nice to you, but you can make sure you behave in a way that makes them feel like being kind to you.

1. Smile

People will be more likely to warm to you and be kind if you smile at them. The chances are, if you give them a genuine smile, one of those that reach your eyes and lights them up, you will get people smiling right back at you.

This will make you appear friendly. Why wouldn't they be kind to you? Also, smiling at another person works on their subconscious mind.

Unless they are really depressed, they will more than likely smile back at you. This helps to relieve any tension they might be feeling and it is usually this tension which makes people be unpleasant with you.

Get rid of their tension and they instantly and instinctively feel like being nice to you because you made them feel good.

2. Be kind to other people

It's an old saying but quite true: "Treat everyone as you would expect to be treated yourself". If you behave respectfully, politely and in a friendly manner toward people then they are much more likely to behave that way toward you.

Behaving in this way sets out your expectations of how you expect people to behave toward you. The vast majority of people, unless they really have an axe to grind with you, will be kind in return.

3. Show a sincere interest

Pay close attention to what people are saying and respond to them in a friendly, supportive manner and they will likely be nice to you. They will like you showing an interest in them and will reciprocate by showing you the same interest so your friendship can develop.

4. Deal with unresolved issues.

Linked to the previous point, if you have history with someone which has unresolved tensions in it which are causing them to be unkind to you, then you might need to address those issues. Do so calmly, rationally and humbly. Recognize and verbalize the issue that is unresolved between you and apologize if you need to. People usually respond well to that.

5. Be a good listener

This goes hand in hand with the previous point. Actively listen to what people are saying and you will find points in their conversation to pick up and develop or ask about. This leads to a good, positive conversation.

6. Make use of a name

This works particularly well to get people to be nice to you if you have only recently met them. Remember their name and mention it in the conversation where appropriate. They will be flattered you remembered it and bothered to use it. It shows them you have energy invested in the conversation.

7. Talk about the other person's interests

In some respects, your job in any conversation is to talk more about the other person than about yourself. Don't worry; their job in the conversation is to talk more about you! So, ask more questions than you make statements.

Find out what makes the other person tick and use that to steer the conversation on to ground in which they feel comfortable. They will then be more likely to do the same for you in other parts of the conversation.

8. Make the other person feel important

The previous point helps a lot with this. By letting them talk about themselves and actively listening to what they tell you this shows the other person that they mean something to you.

How to Get People to Be on Time

It can be infuriating when people are tardy and don't arrive at meetings or social engagements on time. It can make the people who did manage to attend on time feel disrespected and undervalued, even if that kind of feeling is not in the heart of the latecomer.

Often you'll find that the latecomers are the same people every time.

This problem can also spread; if a team at work see that meetings are continually held back for five minutes to allow for the usual suspects to turn up late they start to get the idea that they can also turn up late too and then the problem escalates.

However, you can adopt some simple strategies to get people to be on time.

1. Make punctuality important

The same people who are late for an office meeting that they know will be held up for them perhaps wouldn't dream of turning up late to the theatre or cinema. Maybe that's because they know that these events won't wait for them. So, make your event one that won't be held up for a latecomer either.

You can do this in all kinds of situations. For instance, if you have arranged to meet a friend outside the theatre, and they are late, text the friend to say you've gone into the bar to grab a drink. That way, your own evening has got off to a pleasant start and you're not just hanging around waiting for them.

Added to that, and particularly linked to meetings, is that you must make them useful. If nothing gets decided at your meetings and they are unstructured and confused, there is no real incentive for people to be punctual.

2. Set a reasonable time

People aren't superhuman. If you set a time for a meeting or outing when the people you want to attend will be busy with other things, you are setting yourself up to fail. If you want people to be on time, try to set a mutually convenient time.

3. Once you've agreed a time stick to it

So, If you say the meeting will be at 1pm or that you will meet them outside the theatre at 7pm, do it. Be there yourself. And if they are late, move on: start the meeting or go into the theatre bar to wait for them there. That minimizes the inconvenience to you, and lets them know you are serious about punctuality.

A five minute wait to allow for traffic or unforeseen holdups is excusable, a 20 minute wait while they gussied up or gathered their work papers they didn't organize early enough is not.

4. Convey your expectations

If you say the meeting will start at 1pm, do you mean that is when people should start to arrive at 1pm for coffee and networking? Or does it mean that is when you will be getting down to the business of the meeting.

You can very easily make this clear in an email: "Refreshments 12.30-13.00. Meeting starts 13.00 prompt" or "Delegates should arrive by 1pm. There will then follow an informal meet and greet session after which we will start the meeting."

You can't be disappointed in people not meeting your expectations if you don't make it clear what those expectations are.

5. Make lateness visible

This may sound like a punishment and perhaps it is, but then latecomers to meetings perhaps deserve some kind of punishment. It is work after all!

So, as a latecomer arrives, you may greet them, in a friendly tone, which adds a slightly pointed comment: "Oh hello; come in. I'm afraid you missed getting everyone's names but I'm sure you'll catch up!"

Maybe that slight embarrassment they should feel will make them think twice about being late next time! So, by setting clear and reasonable expectations of punctuality, you can deal effectively with the issue of how to get people to be on time.

How to Get People to Be Quiet

There may be several reasons why you need to know how to get people to be quiet. Perhaps you're about to start a meeting or need to concentrate on some work or another important task; you may even just need some 'me' time! There are many times you want people to speak quieter or to stop talking.

The methods you employ to get people to be quiet will vary according to the situation and your need but it can be done!

1. Don't be rude

This is the golden rule in any situation where you need people to be quiet. You don't want to be seen as rude or the offended person will more than likely spend the next few minutes telling you how rude you are and you will have failed to get them to be quiet.

2. Ask and you may receive

It's just possible that getting someone to be quiet may not be as difficult as you fear. If you politely say "would you mind being quiet because I need to... (whatever your reason is)", sometimes that will work, especially if the person didn't realize they were talking too much or too loudly.

3. Use nonverbal cues

More than fifty per cent of the language we pick up as human beings is nonverbal. These nonverbal cues can be powerful in affecting another person's behavior. And the great benefit is that you are much less likely to appear rude if you use this body language to shut people up than if you had used words, however kind.

So, for instance, if someone is talking too much, you might fix them with a serious stare for a few seconds and when you know they are looking back at you, shake your head disapprovingly. If you have quite a good relationship with the other person or are dealing with children, you might mime zipping your lips. They might even think that is funny but they will get the hint.

If you just need someone to speak in a softer tone, you can hand signal that, too. Use the signal of closing your fingers down against your thumb. This is a quite universal sign of 'quiet down', even used in music.

4. Use humor

This is linked to the last point and works particularly well where you have a good relationship with the other person or people, and where they weren't deliberately being noisy or talking too much.

You could say something as simple as "was that you guys moving around? I thought a herd of baby elephants got in!" or, if you are clearly busy studying, doing paperwork etc. you could try "can you keep the noise down, please; some of us are trying to sleep in here!"

Usually, people will see the funny side of that but it also draws attention neatly to the behavior you want to change.

5. Defer people

Parents will relate well to this one. You get on the phone or in the bath and suddenly your kids have vital things to tell you. Well, then you have something important to teach them: that you can't necessarily drop everything to talk to them unless it's an emergency.

Be calm and friendly. Recognize that it's good they want to talk to them but let them know you are in the middle of something; then comes the most important part: give them a time when you will be able to talk to them.

So, for instance, you might say, "That's a lovely drawing, honey; I've just got to talk to my boss about something and then I'll be right in to look at your picture properly with you..." or similar words that fit the particular situation.

If you do this with a smile and show genuine interest, it usually works, and if it doesn't work the first time, keep on trying; children learn to accept consistency from a loving parent.

This is a selection of techniques you can use to get people to be quiet in a variety of situations.

How to Get People to Believe in You

It can be difficult to get people to believe in you at times. Perhaps you have abused their trust in the past by committing a crime or having an affair. Maybe what you are asking them to trust you on is a dangerous or unlikely proposal. It could be that what you are asking people to trust you on has never been done before, or at least only rarely.

By learning a few strategies, you can discover how to get people to believe in you.

1. Have self belief

If you live your life in integrity, not harming other people and doing good things, you have every right to consider yourself a good, competent person. Having people believe in you starts with your self belief. You should know for yourself that your ideas and actions are positive and then you are in a good frame of mind to convey that feeling to other people.

2. Do as you say you will

If you want people to believe in you, than you must be consistent and trustworthy. If you are the kind of person that sees a project through once you have started and have a proven track record you are more likely to encourage other people to believe in you. Canceling dates, dropping out of arrangements etc. all damage the trust that you want people to build up in you.

3. Tell the truth

Sometimes the truth hurts and at times you might need to sugar coat the pill a little, but you must always be honest if you want people to believe in you. That lets them know they can trust you because they know you will tell them bad news as well as good news. That is important if people are to believe in you.

4. Be clear, never vague

There are many gray areas in life, but sometimes, it is tempting to blur reality even a little more. This burring can be sensed by other people and then little doubts about you creep in because they are not quite sure what you're not telling them.

So, for example, if you are asked something like "How did it go at the doctor's?", don't be tempted to simply say, "Oh fine, he said not to worry", be more truthful and say "It was okay but I haven't got any answers yet; we've got to wait for the test results."

You may feel you are sparing loved ones some worry by giving the first answer, but in reality, you're not; it could be that after your test results you need treatment. If the people you were vague to find out they then may feel hurt and respond, "You said it was nothing to worry about". They will feel like you don't trust them.

Being as clear and honest as you can is always the best way forward. Also, never omit significant details. It is difficult to remember what you have said if you haven't told the whole story and people are likely to find out and feel hurt that you weren't honest with them.

5. Admit when you're keeping something back

Everyone is entitled to privacy, but to get people to believe in you, it's important to put down some clear boundaries about what you are not openly sharing. For instance, you could say "I do have things I feel and think about the divorce, but they aren't things I want to share just now, but you really don't have to worry." People will respect that.

6. Keep other people's secrets

If you are told something in confidence, don't break that trust unless it really is serious. Only then do you divulge a secret, and then only to the people that you absolutely have to tell to avoid danger or harm. Never gossip.

7. Share your feelings

If people know you will open up about what you feel, they will know they can trust you to be open and honest with them. Also, if you only communicate facts and not feelings, you will appear cold and distant. People will find it difficult to trust you if you do that.

These are just some of the behaviors that should become a regular part of life for you if you want to get people to believe in you.

How to Get People to Believe You

Even when you tell the truth sometimes it is difficult to get people to believe you. That is largely because you're not convincing enough. That can be a big problem, particularly at work when you are trying to implement changes or a new project, or at home where you would like to change something about your lifestyle.

It is up to you to be persuasive and here's how to get people to believe you.

1. Believe yourself

This is vitally important if you are to get others to believe you. You must believe in what you are saying or trying to do, to appear authentic. If you don't believe yourself, you have no right to expect others to believe you.

Believing in yourself also allows you to use strong, confident body language that will help to convince people of what you're saying.

2. Understand your audience's beliefs

You need to know what your audience already knows and believes on the topic before you try to convince them of something else. That way, you can work with it, taking people from their present understanding to the new understanding you want them to reach.

Does what you want them to believe agree with their already set ideas or does it contradict those. Naturally, it's more difficult to get people to believe you if what you are telling them contradicts their existing beliefs. This doesn't just refer to religion.

So first, you need to recognize their understanding. For instance, "Suzy and I are splitting up; yeah, I know we always seemed happy together but things have been bad for a while; we just didn't want anyone to know while we tried to work things out but now we feel we're at the end of the road."

3. Give evidence

Two groups of people are particularly hard to convince of anything: experts and skeptics. You can deal with both groups by gathering sound evidence to support your arguments.

Repeat, repeat

Particularly if an idea goes against a person's existing understanding, it is difficult to accept it upon first hearing. Therefore, you may have to tell people something a few times before they believe you.

It could also be that upon repetition, you explain yourself in a slightly different way. Maybe people didn't quite understand you the first time and that is why they didn't believe you.

4. Interact to remove mental barriers

There's no point trying to guess why someone doesn't believe you. Ask them! When you know what the barriers are to them accepting your viewpoint you can work on breaking down those barriers with logic and evidence.

Again, remember to provide evidence to support what you're saying. You may have to undermine the other person's current understanding if it appears to be wrong. However, you need to do this carefully and sensitively. Don't mock them for their beliefs; simply provide evidence that contradicts their beliefs and invite then to answer the challenge that the evidence makes.

5. Speak assertively

The language you use is vital in convincing other people. Use concrete nouns that sound strong. Speak in direct terms and simple sentences that state a case as fact. Use evidence and statistics to back up what you're saying. Help them make a mental picture of your argument.

In this way, you are helping the subconscious minds of your audience to accept what you're saying as already established fact. The subconscious mind can't easily distinguish between fact and fantasy so working on this can be to your advantage when you want to get people to believe you.

How to Get People to Do What You Say

Wouldn't it be great if you knew how to get people to do what you say? Your coworkers would work together seamlessly to follow your orders, your partner would understand and cater for your every whim and your children would obey you instantly.

Well, it's not quite that easy but by adopting a few techniques borrowed from neuro-linguistic programming you can get people to do what you say a lot more of the time than they do now.

1. Understand your audience

First, if you want people to do as you say, you need to understand what makes them tick as an individual. You are going to use psychology on them and for that to work you have to understand what motivates the specific person.

For some people, the glass of life is always half empty, for others it's half full; some people run away from things, others run toward a challenge and attempt to meet it head on. You need to know who you're dealing with first, or if you can't find that out, employ a variety of the following techniques to hit several motivators.

2. Be careful with your wording

"I'll show you how to boost your profits" is the same thing as saying "I'll show you how to beat the recession", but they speak to two quite different types of people.

If you are dealing with people who meet challenges, tell them the first statement; if you are talking to someone who tends to run away, appeal to their need for security and tell them this to protect them from losing money.

Also, you may sugar coat the pill and appeal to the better nature of the person you are requesting something from. Thus, "Honey, I'm tired, could you wash the dishes for me?' is far more likely to get people obeying you than "Hey! Get those dishes washed now!"

3. Show that you know what you're talking about

They need to be able to trust you before they will do what you say. So establish your credentials with your audience. Prove them if necessary. That way, they will see a request that you make of them as sensible and necessary.

4. Flow and association

This is a technique used in psychology, NLP and psychology. That will get the other person unconsciously responding how you want them to respond. You ask a series of 'yes' or 'no' questions, to which the answers are obvious and predictable. When you get a 'yes' answer, smile, and when you get a 'no' answer, frown.

Do this for a series of questions so that you prime the other person to say 'yes', because they subconsciously enjoy making you smile. Then drop in your real request. You are now much more likely to get a positive answer.

5. Appeal to their better nature

It is possible to get someone to do something for you and to make them feel better about themselves in the process. Therefore, you can ask, "Could you hang these curtains for me? You're taller and can reach the rail better". You will have your curtains up in no time and your man feeling ten feet tall and so proud!

6. Be willing to reciprocate

It's not such a good idea to go around issuing orders and expecting people to obey. It will work better if you establish yourself as a team player (even if you're leading that team). Show that you are willing to do your fair share too and then people won't mind helping out when you ask them.

So, by understanding people and employing a few subtle techniques of psychology, you can learn how to get people to do what you say. You have to know what motivates the person you are making the request of but you should also establish yourself as someone worthy of being obeyed. Ask in the right manner and you should get obedience.

How to Get People to Feel Sorry for You

Are you one of those people that others just seem to expect to handle difficult situations? Does your life seem out of control and sometimes inside you're screaming out for someone, anyone, to give you a break?

That can be really hard on a person, and that could be why you need to learn how to get people to feel sorry for you. Once they feel sorry for you, they might help you!

1. Assess your situation

You need to do this honestly as that is the only way to help yourself. It could be that you find that things aren't as bad as you first thought, which should be taken as a positive. However, this reflection could underline to you just how much help you need.

It's important that you don't wallow in self pity. If you want people to feel sorry for you, your situation must warrant it.

2. Talk to the correct person

There is no point trying to get sympathy from someone who can't help you or who doesn't have a clue what you're going through. Instead, try to talk to someone who has experienced the same difficulties as you are going through now. They will also be the most useful ones from whom to seek practical advice.

If there is no-one you know who has gone through the same thing, try talking to a close family member or a trusted friend. Pick someone with whom you can be really honest and with whom you are not afraid to show emotion. They should also be someone who won't judge you or gossip about what you tell them.

2. Pick your time and place

To unburden yourself, you need to feel safe in the place and know that you will not be overheard or interrupted.

3. Be honest
Tell your confidant exactly what is making you feel unhappy and overwhelmed. Don't hold back.

4. Stay calm
This may sound strange advice to stay calm if you want to get people to feel sorry for you. However, it works. You can cry and get emotional, but don't over do it or whine. The idea is that you should appear to be battling bravely with adversity, rather than hosting your own pity party.

5. Show and tell
To get people to feel sorry for you, you must clearly demonstrate how the problems that you are experiencing right now are affecting your life. Tell your confidant how you are feeling (anxious, depressed, angry, isolated, etc.) and how these feelings are affecting your life (lack of sleep, loss of appetite, difficulty in concentrating, etc.).

6. Demonstrate self help
It's important to explain what you have done to help yourself. If people feel you have been lounging around waiting for others to help you, that won't encourage them to feel sympathy for you; they will feel you are trying to manipulate them into solving all your problems for you.

If, on the other hand, you can show that your genuine efforts to help yourself have not worked out, other people will be a lot more sympathetic.

7. Look to the future
Anyone who wants to help you out will not want to be a bottomless pit of help. They won't want you becoming dependent upon them. So, it helps if you can talk through some steps you'd like to take in the future to sort your life out, but explain that you feel too overwhelmed to do it all alone.

That way, they can see the limits of their helping you and they can see that you don't intend to use them and keep on using them. Tell them openly that you want moral and perhaps practical support from them and a listening ear, but that you know that the responsibility for solving your problems lies largely with you.

8. Express gratitude

Everyone likes to be appreciated, so thank your confidant for listening to you and volunteering to help you. Their sympathy will last much longer if they know you appreciate it.

So, the issue of how to get people to feel sorry for you revolves around you convincing them you are in a serious situation and need their help. Then you need to work together with your confidant to solve your problems.

How to Get People to Forgive You

Everyone does something wrong at one time or other in their lives. You may have hurt someone physically or emotionally or broken a trust. But human beings have an immense capacity for forgiveness. If you approach the person you hurt in the right way, you stand a good chance of gaining their forgiveness. However, it does take some work on your part.

Here's some advice on how to get people to forgive you:

1. Forgive yourself

It's a difficult fact for some people to come to terms with but we are all human and we all make mistakes sometimes. It's just who we are. You need to find a way to forgive yourself for what you did and that will allow you to move on and seek the forgiveness of other people.

2. Face up to what you did

It's no good going into denial to forgive yourself. The facts are that you did whatever it was you did and that hurt someone. That won't change just because you deny it but facing up to your guilt will start to make a change.

First, try looking in the mirror and saying: "I know what I did was wrong because..." Next, you should try approaching the person you hurt and admitting your guilt to them to. Don't be scared of that because unless what you did was really bad like a serious crime, the other person is likely to respond well to your approach.

3. Say sorry

It sounds easy to say: "I'm sorry". Yet such simple words can be very difficult to say, especially if you feel guilty. However, it's important to say it if you are ever going to get the other person to forgive you. It's much more unlikely they will forgive you unless you admit guilt and apologize.

4. Give the other person some space

Saying sorry should happen right away after you caused them offense. However, they may not accept it at first. That is why you need to back off after an apology and give the other person time to process it. They will need time to figure out if you were sincere (you better be!) and if they can find it within their heart to forgive you.

5. Stay calm

It can be difficult to keep cool, especially when you have worked yourself up to make an apology, a difficult thing, if it isn't accepted immediately. But don't panic and don't react angrily and blow all your hard work. Very often, in time, they will be willing to listen to you again.

6. Never make excuses

Of course at the time of causing offense you had your reasons for it, but that won't help now. And the fact is that no matter how justified you felt, it is never okay to upset someone. At the very least, you should have tackled things differently to avoid any upset. So never try to excuse your behavior.

7. Let the other person talk

A big part of getting someone to forgive you is for them to feel that you acknowledge the pain you caused them. Therefore, it's important that you let them tell you this. They may get angry, but you must not do the same. Remember, you can't control what they do and they are human too so they may make mistakes; but you are absolutely responsible for how you behave.

8. Be willing to change

It's no good saying sorry now and then carrying on behaving in the same way. Feeling guilty is all about you; it doesn't help the other person or induce forgiveness, but altering your behavior for the better does.

If you have truly examined your own actions, accepted responsibility for them and seen the error of your ways, you should see clearly where and how your behavior needs to change.

Making a positive change speaks volumes to the person your hurt. That way, they can truly see that you are sorry and want to change, so that is a great way to get people to forgive you.

How to Get People to Go Away

Whether it's people wanting you to give to charity or sign their petition when you walk down the street, or your family demanding things of you just as you sit down to an evening's relaxation in front of the TV or an urgent deadline that requires your undivided attention, sometimes you just wish you knew how to get people to go away, don't you?

With the following tips, you can do this and get the time and space you need, without causing too much offense.

1. Avoid eye contact

This method works best when dealing with people in the street that you don't know: strangers asking you to take leaflets, sign a petition etc. Just avoid looking directly at them and keep walking. The vast majority of people won't have the confidence or bad manners to push for contact under these circumstances.

2. Wear headphones

The various personal entertainment devices can be great for avoiding unwanted attention. If you have your headphones on, it will be clear to the other person that you can't easily hear them, so they won't bother talking to you unless it's important.

It works especially well if you also combine it with the previous strategy and don't look directly at people. That makes it especially hard for other people to grab your attention.

3. Scowl

Just as a smile will encourage people to interact with you, a scowl will have the opposite effect. It sends out a message that you are not to be messed with, at least at this time.

The above guidelines are intended particularly for use out on the street, but they will also work at home. However, now let's move on to some methods to get people to go away if you are at home and just want to be left alone for some peace or to get on with something you need to do.

4. Establish some ground rules

This is especially important when you are dealing with children. If you set up your house rules in such a way that a person's bedroom is their sanctuary and that you must knock to enter, and that a closed bedroom door indicates that one does not want to be disturbed, you will find it much easier to get people to go away and leave you in peace.

5. Be honest

Again this works best with family and friends. If you are feeling overwhelmed and don't have the time or energy to deal with all the demands upon you, explain this to the people interrupting you.

6. Strike a deal

After being honest about your need to be left alone, put some limits on it so people can see that you are willing to be reasonable and that there will be a certain point at which you will again be happy to communicate with them and pay attention to what they have to say.

So, for example, you might say, "I really need to get this article written now, but when I've done that I'll come and look through your homework" or something like that. It's not blackmail, it is teaching your children in particular about give and take and compromise. That is a very useful lesson.

7. Get on with what you need to do

Be persistent and do what it is that you set out to do, regardless of interruptions. If you back down now, you will not be taken seriously next time. So, just calmly and in a matter of fact fashion, carry on with your business.

If you get a disgruntled response to this, then just calmly state, "Well, I told you that I need to (do whatever it is that you're doing)". You haven't conned anyone and it's their problem if they didn't listen to or respect what you needed to do.

So, in these ways, no matter what the situation, you can learn how to get people to go away.

How to Get People to Help You

It can be frustrating when you feel that you are getting no help at all and that you have to do everything alone. Sometimes all you want is for other people to pull their weight.

You can't necessarily have a direct impact on the behavior of others, but you can change your behavior to motivate others to help you, and set up a situation where they are expected to help you out.

Here's how to get people to help you

1. Examine your own behavior

Do you make it difficult for people to help you? Are you critical of people's efforts or unclear or ungrateful when people offer to help you? All of these things are guaranteed to make people less likely to want to help you.

So instead, be grateful for help offered and accept that if someone else is doing a task, it might not necessarily get done the way that you'd do it. However, it will get done and you won't have to do it. Be grateful for that!

2. Don't be so available

Moms are especially guilty of this. Their nurturing side takes over and they attempt to do everything that needs to be done for the family, even tasks far above and beyond the call of duty.

That doesn't help your children or your partner. It disempowers them and prevents them from learning vital coping skills. Also, if you are almost constantly available and then suddenly you don't feel like helping out, this can frustrate your family members and make them angry, especially if your anger erupts at them for not doing a task which you have always done.

3. Establish a routine

Just how formal you want to be about this will depend upon your family set up. The point is that household tasks should be divided up. Even quite young children can get a huge sense of achievement by doing small tasks to help out.

Sure at first it might make more work for you as you have to teach them how to do it and supervise. But you and your children can benefit from this far into the future.

4. Don't expect telepathy

It could be that other members of your family simply don't realize a task needs to be done. This can be frustrating in itself but try to remain calm and just say what needs to be done.

5. Ask for help

This point is linked to those above. Even if you have a well established routine, sometimes tasks will crop up that aren't covered. If you need someone to do it for you or at least to help you, ask them. They won't be offended and are more likely to be offended when they see you doing the task later and you hadn't mentioned it.

6. Be assertive yet reasonable

If you have asked someone to do something, you can't necessarily expect them to jump right to it. Very few tasks need doing immediately, and if they do, you should say so. For instance, if you want the kitchen bin emptied because the trash cart is arriving soon, say so.

In the same way, if you want the children to tidy their rooms, set a reasonable time limit (days rather than hours or minutes) in which it needs to be done. Remind them periodically, and stick to your deadline. If it isn't met, impose consequences.

7. Know people's strengths and play to them

Try to make any task a group venture. Allocate tasks according to people's strengths so that they find them easy to do. And play your part too.

Use these techniques to get people to help you, whatever the situation. Try them and see how well they work!

How to Get People to Interact

Whether it's a wedding or a conference, getting a group of people together who don't all know each other can be a tense situation. The biggest worry that any organizer of such an event usually has is that the guests or delegates won't speak to each other. However, even if you are only a small group, getting people to interact can be problematic.

However, there are effective ways to get people to interact.

1. Seating is important

Where and how you seat your guests has a big impact on how they interact. Having no seats and allowing them to walk around probably leads to the most interaction but if they are to eat or write something, this isn't practical. You can either assign seats or have people sit where they want to.

There are pros and cons on both sides. If people choose their seats, they will probably sit with people they know and interact with them but probably won't mingle outside of that group. If you assign seats, it is a big responsibility for you if neighbors don't get on and it can go badly or well, depending on how shy people are about talking to strangers.

If you want to set up a small scale interaction at home, you should use some comfortable chairs. Place them at angles to each other and close together. The closeness breeds empathy but face to face would seem confrontational.

Set up different displays, food stations or bars

This is suitable for large group gatherings like weddings and conferences and fulfills two functions which will help people interact. First, they have to get up and move to them so they walk past other people; this encourages them to interact. Also, once they get there they have a common purpose with the other people standing in that area so it gives them something to talk about.

2. Introductions

At a meeting with a reasonably small group of people, ask people to introduce themselves briefly. They don't have to say much but it helps people to start making connections.

If you are with a few people you know but who don't know each other you could break the ice for everyone by making the introductions. You could also make these funny and ease the tension, but be careful not to embarrass anyone or make them feel awkward.

3. Names

Give people name badges to wear. Make sure they are clearly written. Others feel more comfortable speaking to people if they know the name of the person to whom they are speaking.

4. Set up group activities

This is a suitable technique for many conferences and work gatherings. If people have to work together to achieve an aim they have to interact. Do this quite early in the day and you will have broken the ice so that they continue interacting throughout the day.

5. Build the atmosphere

People won't talk if they feel threatened, so you need to establish a relaxed environment in which they can interact. You may have to set ground rules at the beginning of the conference so that people know they will be listened to and their contributions respected.

6. Get rid of distractions

This may entail moving to a private room where you aren't going to be interrupted. If you are at home and want to get some family interaction, you should turn off the TV and perhaps even the phone if the discussion is important enough. That will allow everyone to concentrate fully on the interaction.

So, there are some proven methods to get people to interact. Some rely on setting up the event well and take a little preparation; others happen throughout the event but just require a little empathy and encouragement of the interaction.

How to Get People to Invite You to Places

Does your social life need a kick start? Are you tired of staying in every night or going to the same old places with the same old people? You need to know how to get people to invite you to places.

1. Look like the kind of person who people want to invite out

This begins with the basics of good personal hygiene and dressing appropriately. You will be much more likely to be asked to places if your appearance isn't an embarrassment or off-putting to the people who might invite you.

2. Get to know more people

The most common way to meet people is through work or a hobby, so if you want to get to know more people you should consider taking up a new hobby or joining a new club. Shared interests are a great way to get to know new people and explore new activities together.

3. Take the initiative

You don't have to wait for someone else to invite you out; you could issue the invitation yourself. It can be a casual drink after work or a group outing to the races; it can be anything, so long as you find a group of like-minded people who want to do it.

4. Make it a good experience

Once you have got an invitation to go out with a new friend or group of friends, you have to ensure that they like being with you enough to want to go out with you again. So, don't make a fool of yourself; wear appropriate clothes, control your alcohol intake and behave in a suitable manner. Definitely don't get drunk until you know people very well and you know how they would react to this.

Don't flirt with other people until you understand the dynamics. It isn't appropriate on the first few meetings anyway, but even after that, you need to be sure of the other person's sexuality, know whether they are already in a relationship etc.

5. Don't monopolize the conversation

It can get boring if your companions are spending the whole time listening to you talk. If you are invited out, you want to make it fun, so be careful to also ask appropriate questions of your companions. More importantly, listen to the answers and respond accordingly so that you have a truly interactive conversation.

6. Avoid contentious subjects

Until you know people better, don't talk about subjects such as religion and politics. You might not know what their views on the subjects are and you don't want to risk offending people and making a scene by airing unpopular views. That isn't the way to get invited out again!

7. Be a good guest

If you are invited to a larger event, such as a party, make sure you circulate. That will give you a chance to meet even more new people and get even more invitations; also, it will mean that you don't monopolize the attention of certain guests, such as the ones you know.

This is good because you don't want to appear needy if you want to get more invitations.

8. Share your interests

You can't expect new friends to be mind readers. If you don't let them know what you're interested in, they can't know. If you tell them your interests, you might find they tell you about a whole range of different invitations and then your circle of friends will be widened even further.

So, it isn't that difficult to know how to get people to invite you to places. You just have to let them know the kinds of invitations that you would like and be a good guest when you are asked out.

How to Get People to Like You More

If you are wondering how to get people to like you more, you probably suffer from low self esteem, and feel that other people don't like you very much. The chances are that this is a false impression and that at least some people like you a lot more than you like yourself.

However, we can all do with a self esteem boost, so here are some techniques to get people to like you more.

1. Allow people to connect with you

This doesn't mean making connections on the latest social networking site; it means in your regular daily life. Allow others to get close to you and to get to know the real you, without putting up defensive barriers against this.

2. Develop empathy with other people

As you let others get close to you and know the real you, take the time to get to know other people well too.

Put yourself in the other person's shoes and see how the world looks from their point of view. Experience their emotions with them and you will undoubtedly develop a deeper connection.

3. Be reliable

Be someone that others can rely on in a crisis or at a difficult time in their lives. This means you need to be there for people when they feel they need it, not just when you can be bothered to make the effort.

You can either provide practical or emotional support or you can help them get the professional help they need like finding them the phone number of an out of hours plumber.

4. Give people your undivided attention

Everyone likes to feel that they are the center of the universe, so make them the center of your universe, even if it's only for a few minutes. Concentrate on the other person totally and on what they are saying and doing.

5. Give people what they need

This may be a hug, some encouraging words or someone's shoulder to cry on. Whatever it is that the other person needs, if you can be the one to give it to them, they will like you more.

6. Be kind and understanding

Don't criticize. Be polite and accept other people for who they are. Life doesn't have to be your one person crusade to change others and this usually fails anyway. Just accept people for who they are and they will like you more.

7. Notice the small things

Everyone feels good when other people notice the minor details about them like having lost weight or got a hair cut. Compliment them on these things and they will feel great, and as a consequence, because you were the one who made them feel that way, they will like you more.

8. Put yourself out for people

Offer them a lift if they are having car trouble; hold the ladders for them if they are hanging curtains; cook them a meal if they are feeling ill yet have a family to cater for. It doesn't have to be a big thing, but your effort will be appreciated.

9. Be a good listener

Sometimes, what people want more than anything else is a person they can trust to offload their troubles. If that is you, they will like you a lot more. You must be trustworthy and not judge or break confidences, but otherwise, being a good listener costs you hardly any effort at all.

So, these tips have shown you how to get people to like you more. Most of the tips are surprisingly easy to implement and what is really most important is that you respond to what the other person needs from you and that you are there for them to help in bad times as well as being there to celebrate the good times.

How to Get People to Listen to You

It can be really frustrating when you have something that you want to say if people don't take any notice of you. However, if you are saying the right things at the right time in the right way, you can make great progress and get people to listen to you.

1. Make sure you have the correct information

Nobody will want to listen to you if you are trying to tell them something they know or suspect to be wrong. Check your facts first before you try to present them.

2. Pick the right time

You will be aware that there are times when you are just too busy or hurried to take on board any new information. It is the same scenario for everyone else in the world too. So, if you need to tell somebody something important, don't tell them just as they are leaving the office or about to set off for work, or when they are trying to cook dinner for the family.

They just won't physically be capable of listening to you properly at that point and you will be wasting their time and yours.

3. Select a good situation

Do you need to have privacy for when you tell the other person what you need to tell them? If so, ensure that you get the privacy and don't just jump at the first opportunity you get to talk to them.

Maybe you need to arrange to have the kids babysat while you talk properly with your spouse. Again, arrange it properly and take the stress out of the situation.

4. Avoid distractions

This is linked to the previous point and is particularly pertinent where it is serious or bad news which you need to pass on to the other person. Switch off the TV and get away from other people in order to be able to talk effectively one-on-one.

If you want people to listen to you at a conference or meeting, you should also cut out distractions. Make sure that people not connected to the meeting will not wander into the room and interrupt. Put up a 'Do Not Disturb' sign if necessary. Switch off noisy fans or lights which buzz.

5. Don't distract your listeners

You carry much of the responsibility for whether or not someone listens to you attentively. So, don't exhibit annoying mannerisms like fiddling with your sleeves or collar, even if you're nervous. If you do, that is what your audience will remember, not what you said to them.

6. Don't talk for too long

If you are speaking to people, be aware that they will take in much less information than they can read. So don't talk for long. Fifteen minutes maximum is the longest time that most adults can listen to an oral presentation without getting distracted and for children it is much less time.

7. Make your message clear

Make sure you present a logical argument, with all your points in the correct order. Keep your sentences short and direct.

8. Pause

Every few sentences, you should stop and look at you audience. This allows you to judge how well the audience is receiving your words. More importantly, it allows the listeners to catch up with you and process what you're saying. Listening attentively is hard work so they need the occasional break or their brains will just switch off whether you want them to or not.

9. Be good to listen to

Vary your tone of voice in volume and pitch to make your presentation interesting. You can also use these techniques to draw attention to specific parts of the speech.

If you follow these steps to get people to listen to you, you should get an attentive audience, no matter how big or small. That will enable you to effectively get your point across to your listeners.

How to Get People to Meet Deadlines

This can be a frustrating and difficult situation. This is especially true if you are part of a team of workers and you are reliant on other people doing their work on time before you can do your own job or to get the project completed.

This is a particular difficult situation because when you are considering how to get people to meet deadlines then you are looking at ways to influence another human being, which is not always possible and usually isn't easy.

However, there are certain tactics you can use to help other people to meet deadlines.

1. Make sure that the work is within the capability of the other person

Any deadline, no matter how generous, is destined to be missed if the person to whom a task has been allocated is unable to do the work. So, you need to know the person well enough to give them, the right kinds of jobs.

2. Make deadlines realistic

A deadline which is too near, rather than motivating someone to work harder will be more likely to make them panic. When people panic they can't think effectively so obviously they then can't work effectively and that puts the deadline even further in jeopardy.

A good rule of thumb might be for you to think seriously about how long it would take you personally to do the work and try to set a deadline with that in mind, if possible.

3. Involve the person in making their own deadline

You may not be fully aware of the entire workload of the person for whom you are setting a deadline, so if you do this unilaterally you may be unrealistic and unfair.

So, take some time to sit down with the other person in a calm environment. Discuss with them what their workload is and ask them to suggest a deadline by which they feel they can get the work done.

Be aware that they may try to please you by saying an optimistic deadline, so you may want to ask some supplementary questions like: what other work have you got to do and when is it due? Does that deadline give you a realistic break or is it going to result in you getting burned out and exhausted?

4. Help them to break down the task into smaller parts

This can and should be done at the interim stage of deadline setting. Point out what work would need to be done on a daily or weekly basis to meet that deadline, and therefore how much time must be devoted to that project each day. Ask them if they feel they can realistically commit themselves to doing that.

5. Set interim deadlines

Once you have discussed a deadline and decided how the work needs to be apportioned in time, you can set some interim deadlines so that the other person knows what part of the project they should be focusing on. This way the task becomes less overwhelming.

6. Discuss progress regularly

Progress should be assessed and every interims deadline date agreed on. You also need to see hard, factual evidence of the progress.

Has the work assigned for that section of the project time been completed? If so, great and that will boost the worker's confidence and given them the motivation to move on.

If not, why not? What were the problems and how can they be solved or avoided in the future? Does the deadline need to be reassessed in view of these problems at an interim stage?

7. Be approachable

In order for a worker to feel comfortable undertaking this planning with you and letting you know where they are not meeting their interim deadline targets, you need to make yourself approachable. Don't get angry at a missed deadline; instead, discuss the reasons for it and be supportive. Help the worker move on and progress.

In this way, You can be a friendly and supportive manager with the best approach to get people to meet deadlines. And of course these principles also apply at home.

How to Get People to Mind Their Own Business

With all the reality TV and fly on the wall documentaries we see these days, it's no wonder that some people can't see that real life should be different and so they continually stick their noses in other people's business. However, you don't have to tolerate this. You do have a right to privacy and here is how you can exercise that right.

1. Don't do anything in which the authorities should take an interest

Okay, so this is starting with an obvious point, but if you beat a child, steal someone else's property or mistreat an animal you really don't deserve the right to privacy on that particular issue.

So, let's say you live a legal, relatively blameless life. How can you protect your right to privacy and prevent other people interfering in your life?

2. Don't make your private life public knowledge

Celebrities are great ones for doing this. They sell photographs to everything from weddings to childbirth to cosmetic surgery, and then they get upset when people come up to them in the supermarket for autographs. What can they expect once they have blurred the lines of acceptability so much?

Now, unless you're a celebrity reading this article, you are unlikely to have anyone asking for your autograph over the frozen pizzas, still this advice is good for you too. If you don't want anyone talking about your marriage problems then don't kiss another woman in the bar, for example.

3. Be discreet

If you're having an affair with your secretary and you don't want word to get around, don't flirt in the office. Remain professional and keep your personal life out of work hours and out of the office.

4. Guard your personal correspondence

Of course, people should never read your private letters but you can be sure that if you leave such items lying around then some unscrupulous person will be sure to read them. For that reason, you should keep your email password protected and never tell anyone else your password.

5. Don't fuel suspicions with secretive behavior

This might sound like the opposite of the advice given so far but really it isn't. It's just that if you have nothing to hide, you shouldn't act like you have. You may enjoy having a slight air of mystery about you for a while but this can backfire badly. You may appear untrustworthy and you may be the subject of some nasty gossip about what your secret could be.

6. Make some preemptive strikes

If you are having some work done at home, a new kitchen fitted, or a new dishwasher delivered let your neighbors know, in passing. They will see the cardboard boxes arrive and if you don't want them flapping their gums about what could be in those packages, just tell them. If it's no big deal to you, you will have stolen all their thunder and there won't be any point talking about it behind your back.

7. Behave appropriately in public

If you don't want people talking about you behind your back, don't give them any bad behavior to talk about.

8. Learn how to deal with intrusive questioning

Without causing offense, avoid answering any questions that you don't want to answer. Make an excuse to get out of the situation, even if it is a lie. Smile and excuse yourself, saying that you need to head off to a dental appointment or to pick up the kids.

If the other person already knows that you are having problems but you don't want to discuss them, then smile and thank them for their concern but state simply that the situation is under control and you really don't want to talk about it.

These methods to get people to mind their own business should be effective if applied calmly and consistently with the people who seem to want to interfere in your life.

How to Get People to Not Make Fun of You

Unfortunately, some people believe that making fun of people is entertaining and sometimes even the people who are being made fun of will have a laugh and a joke about it so that they do not feel stupid or hurt. This is usually, however, far from the truth and it is the psychological damage that does the real harm.

Of course there is no simple solution to this problem but there are certain things that will help to stop people making fun of you:

1. We need to understand why some people may make fun of you. Most people who bully believe that they are stronger or better in certain ways than you are. They believe that they can control you or gain certain advantages over you which make them feel better about themselves. For as long as these bullies keep thriving on these conditions it is unlikely that they will stop.

2. If you take away their attention seeking control that they believe they achieve while bullying people then you take away the need to do it at all. By this we mean that if you were to ignore them then their bullying becomes a pointless task as they do not gain from it, so just ignore them.

3. When you are ignoring people who make fun of you, you should remember that there are certain ways to go about it. First your body language should be tall and proud. If you look like they are getting to you then they will keep on making fun at you.

4. Another must is that you do not make eye contact when you are being subjected to verbal abuse as this shows that you have paid some attention to what was being said and they could persist.

5. Always try to remember never to talk back to them as this can lead to them becoming more aggressive and the bullying could get out of hand leading to possible violence. By ignoring them completely this will take all the fun the bully has out of bullying and they will leave you alone.

6. Remember to be confident as some people who are perceived as weaker or as some would class loner are the main targets to bullies. They are seen as easy prey and will usually get the attention of bullies.

7. When you are the subject of someone making fun of you, always remember to speak clearly and never to act timid or shy as this can also lead to you becoming a target to people who are looking for someone to bully.

8. Most people at some point in their lives will suffer from some sort of verbal abuse. This unfortunately is the way that human life is but you should not take anything that is said to heart as this is exactly what they want.

9. Even if they are making fun of you because of something that bothers you, like obesity or a disability, do not let them see that it bothers you as this can cause an escalation in the bullying.

10. If you portray to others that you are a confident person then chances are you will not be a target for bullies as they will see you as a threat who may give back as good as he or she gets.

11. Although it is easier said than done, ignoring bullies who make fun of you can still have an emotional impact on people and it is because of this that you should make sure that you can confide in people who you trust about the problems. Keeping them bubbled up inside can lead to unnecessary stress and can have an negative effect of your life.

12. Always try to associate yourself with a group of people who can be classed as your friends. It is a lot harder to bully a group of people than an individual.

Unfortunately, bullying is common especially in schools and among the younger members of society but you can learn how to get people to not make fun of you. If you follow these steps then they can help you from becoming a target or getting them to stop altogether.

How to Get People to Notice You

Whatever you are doing, either professionally or socially, if it is a good thing, it feels special if people notice you, doesn't it? But all too often, people's efforts go unnoticed. However, you can change all that and learn how to get people to notice you, whether that is in a social situation or in the workplace.

Let's begin by considering how to get people to notice you in a social setting, because most, if not all of these factors are also applicable to the workplace too. You still want to attract the attention of human beings and they work pretty much the same way whatever setting they are in, when it comes to what attracts their attention.

1. Smile

To attract positive attention, you need, most importantly, not to scare away that attention. Do not glare and make yourself look intimidating as people will be scared to approach you and they will ignore you to protect themselves. So, smile. Make the smile go all the way to your eyes so that you appear genuinely happy and welcoming of attention.

2. Appear confident yet not arrogant

This is hugely important. People don't want to involve themselves with those who will be needy and hard work. So, hold your head up, put your shoulders back and look like someone with a comfortable sense of self worth. This will make you look like more fun to communicate with, so people will be more likely to approach you.

3. Don't look desperate for company or attention

This can attract the wrong kind of attention and cause you a lot of problems with people who are equally needy or who are predators willing to suck up what little self worth you have left.

Instead, appear comfortable in your own skin. People will perceive you then as not being high maintenance and so, ironically perhaps, they will be more likely to give you attention.

4. Make eye contact

Just scope the room until you find someone's eyes to lock on to for a few moments. Then work that smile again. The chances are that they will want to approach you and strike up a conversation.

5. Speak to someone

If you want to be noticed, talk to the person you want to be noticed by. Of course, don't creep them out by throwing yourself at them and declaring your undying love for them. But make a casual, positive comment about the event that brings you two together today.

These methods will all help you to get noticed for the right reasons. They work well in social and work situations, whether you are with strangers or with people that you know better. Now let's look more specifically at how to get noticed in a work situation.

6. Do your job to the best of your ability

You don't want to be the one who gets noticed for constantly letting team members down, breaking the Xerox machine or constantly calling the IT department for help, do you? If you do your job well, people will start to notice and you will start to get praise. That should boost your confidence and make you feel more comfortable about attracting other attention.

7. Be a good team member

If you help other people out when you can people will be appreciative of that and will start to notice your efforts a lot more. This also works with your friends and family.

8. Make a positive contribution

You don't need to be the team leader or the most productive person in your office to make a positive contribution. Just have the confidence to speak up with your own ideas or to support the ideas of other people.

This will help you with the next point too...

9. Form allegiances
Often it is easier to try to get yourself noticed when you feel confident that your ideas will be met with positivity. So try out ideas on a few people at first. If they are well received, perhaps go with one of your allies to put your ideas to your manager.

All of these techniques will help you to get people to notice you for all the right reasons, whether this is at home or at work.

How to Get People to Open up

Sometimes you can tell that a friend, family member or loved one is deeply troubled. If you know someone well, changes in their normal behavior are a good indication that something is bothering them. If you truly care about them, it might help them to talk it through, but it is not always easy to know how to get people to open up to you.

The following are a few tips to get someone you care about to confide their troubles:

1. Gain the other person's confidence

One way of doing this might be to share something about yourself with them. If you open up to them, they might reciprocate. If you have had a long relationship with the other person, and felt that you already trusted one another completely, you might be puzzled, or even offended, that they have not already confided in you.

Perhaps they are reluctant to burden you with their problems? If you suspect this is the case, you should approach them quietly, tell them that you know something is bothering them, and reassure them that you are there for them if they need somebody to talk to.

2. Let the person know that you truly care about them, and that you are not just being intrusive

Make them see that you are ready to help. Assure them that you are not going to be judgmental, and won't be shocked by whatever they tell you.

3. Be prepared to be patient

The other person might not be ready yet to open up to anyone, so don't try to force things. Just be there for them when they are ready to confide.

4. Choose a good place and time

Once the person is ready to confide, choose a suitable time and location to sit and talk. It should be somewhere you are not going to be overheard, or constantly interrupted, and you should allow sufficient time so that your friend does not feel pressured.

5. Make sure that you really listen to what they are saying

Lean towards them and make lots of eye contact to show that you are interested, and nod to demonstrate that you are following their account. Don't interrupt, but let them maintain their flow, so that they can get things out of their system.

6. Give some sensitive prompts

If your friend is finding it difficult to express what they want to say, you could try to prompt them with a few gentle, yet probing questions, or make comments that move the conversation forward.

Ask open questions that require more than a yes or no response, and keep your tone quiet and reassuring. Don't be afraid to let your friend be silent for a few moments though. They might need time to compose their thoughts, so be sensitive and don't push too hard.

7. Don't judge

After you have heard what the other person has to say, you must then ensure that you are not judgmental about what they have revealed, and don't, under any circumstances criticize their behavior, or else they will instantly clam up against you. Remain supportive and sympathetic.

8. Give some practical help

If there isn't anything that you can do, remind them that you are always there for them, and that they can feel free to open up to you any time they are feeling low. Knowing that they have a friend to confide in will be a weight off their minds, and talking things over can sometimes be the first step to healing.

So, to get someone close to open up to you, you need to be supportive, tactful, discreet and not judgmental. Remind the other person that you are always there to lend an ear when they are troubled, and never betray their confidence.

How to Get People to Pay Attention to You

No one likes to feel that they are being ignored. It shows disrespect and it is hurtful. However, on the other hand, being the center of attention and grabbing all the limelight might not be your thing either.

So how do you learn how to get people pay attention to you: the correct, positive kind of helpful attention that gives you respect and says that you are worthy of taking notice of?

1. Be genuine

Most people can spot a fake. That doesn't create respect. You need to have the confidence to be yourself and feel that you are worthy of respect for who you genuinely are.

Relax and show your personality, and don't try too hard to impress as that will only lose you respect. People will pay you a lot more respect if they understand who you are and they know you will stick to that with integrity.

2. Develop yourself

Having just stated that you need to be genuine, it is also important to note that you must be worthy of people's time if you want them to pay attention to you. So, if you don't have much in the way of knowledge or conversation skills, learn them. Everyone has skills to learn in life and this will help you a lot in getting people to pay attention to you.

3. Develop your social skills

Sometimes, whether people will pay attention to you is more to do with the delivery than the message. Practice speaking clearly and confidently and putting some intonation into your voice. This helps people to make sense of what you say and makes you more interesting to listen to.

4. Be honest

You can't expect people to pay attention to you if they feel they can't trust you. Therefore, you should always be honest. Lying usually gets discovered and if people think you are a liar they will be less likely to pay attention to you in the future.

5. Say useful things

Related to the previous point, if you really expect people to pay attention to you, you need to tell them useful things. This entails you seeing things from the point of view of the person you are talking to. What do they need to know from you and what will they not accept hearing from you?

Of course, you stand a much greater chance of people paying attention to you if you tell them things they need to and want to know. That doesn't mean lying to them of course but if you really must tell someone something they don't want to know, then you may need to sugar coat the pill a little.

6. Be tactful

Be sensitive and don't make your words a personal attack. If possible, always say something positive which will leave the person feeling good. Where you must criticize, be constructive and give the person something clear that they need to change or improve.

7. Set the scene

There are many distractions in day to day life and some of those distractions occur in people's own heads. To get people to pay attention to you, you may need to set the scene a little.

At a formal meeting or presentation, insist that cell phones are switched off. Maybe even close the curtains. Even for a more informal communication, if you have something important to say, take the person you are talking to aside to a private, quiet place where you both feel safe and comfortable but where you won't be distracted.

This is particularly important if you will need to give constructive criticism or bad news.

So, it is up to you to get people to pay attention to you. Be a person worthy of respect; make sure you are saying something important and useful and that you deliver your message appropriately, if necessary setting the scene for where you must communicate.

How to Get People to Respect You

In everyday life there are two different kinds of respect that you can get from those you interact with, earned respect and normative respect. However, the respect you get from other people is largely a result of the way that you behave. You can control how to get people to respect you.

The first type of respect is earned respect and involves emotions like love and admiration. Earned respect takes time to cultivate and is based on qualities like confidence, trustworthiness, values, and the beliefs of the person that is respected. Earned respect is based more on the knowing of someone over a long time.

Normative respect is the other kind of respect that is given to someone and is the most common type of respect that people give to people that they don't know. For example, a man may open a door for a woman he doesn't know.

Normative respect is also a respect given because of a person's status, not necessarily for the kind of person they are. For example, most people have respect for a police officer, the law, or for their boss. Normative respect is based more on duty.

Right now, we are mainly concerned with earned respect.

In the workplace, the family home or in everyday life, the ideal type of respect to gain from your peers, managers and employees is of course earned respect. However, if you are a manager or supervisor you will gain normative respect from most of your employees because of your status. But, as was indicated earlier, earned respect takes time to acquire because it involves the demonstration of behaviors and attitudes.

Let's look at some ways to gain earned respect.

1. Talk Less and Listen More

Rather than talking about how good you are something (which just sounds like boasting), show other people how good you are in your actions. If you are behaving in the right way you won't need to justify your actions.

Additionally, you don't need to speak up about every little thing that takes place around you. Be selective about what things are worthy of your opinion.

Everybody likes to be heard and when you patiently listen to those talking to you, then you are showing your interest, concern and appreciation for them. Moreover, listening is complimentary to talking. When you thoroughly listen to someone you become more able to properly influence them when you do talk.

2. Show Sincere Appreciation

Sincere appreciation and flattery are two quite different things. You might use flattery on someone at the local bar to get their attention to let them know you are interested in them. Sincere appreciation, on the other hand, is not about receiving a reciprocal response. It's about recognizing good behaviors and actions in another person and complimenting them for it in a genuine manner. When you see people around you who deserve appreciation, you should give it generously and without flattery. They will respect you for it

3. Honesty

If you are dishonest or untruthful you will never gain genuine respect from the people around you. If you are dishonest they may give you normative respect because of your position but you will never earn real respect. If something goes wrong and you are responsible, step up and take that responsibility without shifting the blame elsewhere. You will be much better respected for it in the long term.

4. Have Self Respect

Having self respect is perhaps the most important component of earning respect from others. Without self respect, there is no way you can respect others and behave in ways to earn their respect in turn.

So, knowing the difference between the two kinds of respect, normative and earned, you can also gain an understanding of some ways to gain genuine respect in your life. By applying these tips in your daily life you can easily find yourself much more respected, and as a result, much happier.

How to Get People to Shut up

Some people talk just to hear themselves talk, while others have to explain every detail of their lives. Some people never seem to shut up, no matter whether they are monopolizing the conversation or you have a meeting to start or whatever.

You will no doubt be familiar with these people because they are also the ones who can never let you finish your story before they unkindly interrupt you with a similar story that, to them, is even better.

However the person is talking to much, you can get them to shut up. You need to, if you are going to get them to listen to you.

People who can't shut up generally just ramble on from subject to subject, even when the subject they are bouncing to has no relevance to the topic that is being talked about. These folks can be some of the most irritating people to be socializing with. They can, in a real sense, put a damper on an otherwise an enjoyable time, so to save you a lot of frustration you need to know how to cope with them.

To get people to shut up can be a challenge, but it can be done. Here are some ideas that should help you.

1. Be serious

Be serious without trying to offend when letting the person who can't shut up know that they need to shut up. They need to know that you really want them to be quiet, but if you offend them it could be counterproductive, making them angry and aggressive and ultimately more of a problem than just talking a lot.

2. Body language

There are many body language signals you can send, along with gentle comments that could send the message, "Please shut up", to the person who talks too much. If you are good enough about subtly letting them know enough is enough, you could save them some embarrassment, which would naturally offend them.

3. Try staring for a few seconds

Just stare at people who can't seem to shut up to help them get the idea that they should stop talking. A good stare, with a serious expression on your face, will let them know that you are tired of listening to their noise.

4. Ignore them

This a powerful message to send to a person who just can't keep their lips from flapping. The disadvantage to ignoring anyone is that it is always taken as an offense.

5. Don't laugh at the jokes of the people that you want to shut up

Don't give them this approval, because it only gives them fuel and energy to keep talking since now people are laughing because of them.

Fortunately, most people who can't shut up do catch on to the ignoring, the stares, and the lack of laughter at their jokes as a time to really shut up or exit stage left.

6. Walk away when nothing else works in shutting someone up

There is only so much any of us can take if we are faced with someone who just won't shut up. When someone who is talking too much is really getting on your nerves you have two choices. The first is to confront them, which then can turn into something neither of you want, if you don't implement the above steps very carefully with tact and diplomacy.

Or you can take the difficult option, but sometimes the right choice, and walk away. This may be your only choice if you are worried that tackling the person any other way would provoke them to anger. That would help no one.

Getting people to shut up is not all that easy at times. People who talk a lot can really get on your nerves and they can very hard to be around. Use these tips and these difficult people will be easier to handle.

How to Get People to Take You Seriously

Even world leaders are not taken seriously all the time. However, when people are not taking you seriously there are some things you can do to let them know that you are serious and that they should respect you.

Here are some easy to apply tips to get people to take you seriously.

1. Stand your ground if you deeply believe in what you are serious about

There will be people who will say that what you are serious about is nothing more than a joke; this will be especially true when those, with that negativity, don't have all the facts. It could be that you know better than your doubters.

Nonetheless, you may well find yourself having to make a stand if it means that much to you. So people know you are serious, you must take a stand and hold that ground no matter what if you have a belief in what you want taken seriously.

Often when you hold your ground the other person might eventually see what you are trying to say to them. If not, still hold on to how earnest you are about whatever you want to be taken seriously.

2. Be assertive in letting people know you are serious

If you are wishy-washy about anything you think you are serious about, it sends a message that you are not that serious about anything, which then of course speaks to your integrity.

So know what you are serious about and assert yourself in ways consistent with your belief. Think of being yourself and standing on the rock of who you are, and for what you believe in, and you will become assertive.

3. Have passion for what is important to you and that passion will let people know that you are serious.

For example, if you are committed to helping society in some specific way, have a passion for that and people will see that you are serious about what you want to do.

4. Your behavior will send many signals of how sincere you are.

If you are always goofing off and clowning around then it will make it difficult for people to take you seriously. If you think you are a 'player' and behave like that not many people will be able to take you seriously.

If you sacrifice your dignity to be the center of attention you send the message that you have no personal values which you hold dear. A person without personal values is not a serious person. Your behavior speaks loudly and will have an effect on how seriously people will take you.

5. What you say and how you say it is another indicator of how serious you are.

Your words and behavior are intimately intertwined. If you say one thing and then do another then there will be a likely chance that no one will be able to take you seriously.

Be consistent in your word and action if you want people to take you seriously.

How you say things is another sign of how serious you are. If you boisterously walk around saying you are going to this and that, without taking action to make things happen, not only will you be seen as not being serious, but obnoxious as well.

Serious people don't need to advertise it to know they are serious. They are action oriented.

Getting people to take you seriously is ultimately up to you, especially how seriously you take yourself. You have now been given a few practical points on how to get people to take you seriously. Use them and you will find more people treat you with respect and admiration.

How to Get People to Talk about Themselves

How do you get people to talk about themselves? Most people like to talk about themselves and what is going on in their lives with those around them. By sharing things about oneself with others it gives one an opportunity for growth.

However, there are those people that shy away from the idea of talking about themselves, but with sensitivity, they can be helped to open up.

There could be any one reason, or a combination of reasons, that make some people reluctant to share personal information with those they interact with. However, there are some things you can do to help encourage people to talk about themselves if you're interested in getting to know them more.

Here are some ideas to get people to talk about themselves.

1. Listen properly to what is being said

When trying to get people to talk about themselves. Often, you will discover, hidden in their conversation, points that can be an opportunity to get someone to talk more about themselves.

For example, asking pertinent and connecting questions that are appropriate to what the other is talking about, is a good way to gain someone's confidence so they open up to you more. Asking appropriate questions, at them right time, lets the other person know that you are listening to them.

Listening builds confidence between people and encourages people to talk about themselves.

2. Take your time

Don't try to rush in getting someone to confide in you if you are really interested in getting to know that person.

Most people don't feel comfortable with telling a stranger about themselves. In fact, it could be dangerous to do that in today's world. So don't rush it.

The point is this: it takes time to build trust and confidence in order for people to feel comfortable enough to exchange the details of their lives. It's part of how relationships grow over time.

3. Make eye contact with the person that you are trying to get to talk about themselves

Eye contact indicates one is sincere, but your eyes also send messages of understanding and compassion. It is those eyes that could help someone talk to you more easily about themselves.

Eye contact allows you to see the emotions of the other person and them to see ours There's a special connection which happens when you look each other in the eye.

In addition, eye contact is an encouraging way to get people to talk about themselves. It shows you care.

4. Use genuine facial expressions in combination with your eye contact

Your facial expressions reinforce the sincerity and compassion of your eyes. A gentle smile mixed with understanding and eyes of compassion can comfort others so that they can relax and trust you. That helps them talk about themselves with you.

In the same way, facial expressions of shock and disapproval can cause someone to stop sharing their life experience with you in an instant.

5. Don't take it personally if someone does not want to talk to you about themselves.

First, it's just the way it is with some people. Accept it as a natural part of human nature.

Also, keep in mind that just because someone doesn't want to talk to you about themselves doesn't mean they don't want to talk to you about anything else, perhaps even about you. Think about that. If you go with the flow, they may feel comfortable talking about themselves with you in the future.

Knowing how to get people to talk about themselves is not about you, but them. By using the ideas given above you might be able to encourage people you care about to talk about themselves with you. And if someone doesn't want to talk about themselves with you, that's okay too.

How to Get People to Talk to You

Knowing how to get people to talk to you can be a bit of an awkward experience, especially during times when you are first getting to know a person. With time and familiarity, it becomes easier, but in the early days of communication with a person, it can pose problems.

For example, imagine you find yourself sitting next to a person and you each have acknowledged each other's presence. Then you might introduce yourself; they do likewise, but from there the conversation kind of dwindles off, except for giving occasional glances to each other and thoughts of who is going to make the next move.

Fortunately for you, you can easily learn how to get people to talk to you. Picking up on the body language that they don't just want to be left alone and might welcome communication, is a good start.

1. Use eye contact

Maintain eye contact with the person you are trying to talk to, even when you sense a lull in the conversation. Eye contact tells the other person that you are still connected to them and are interested in talking with them.

When people sense that you want to talk to them they will, more than likely, want to talk to you.

2. Greet the person you want to talk to

For example, if you want to talk to a person while you both wait for an appointment then greet them. Say, "Hi" to them and maybe even make a comment about how enjoyable it is for you to meet them. You will be surprised how many people will want to talk to you when you greet them the right way.

3. Smiling is another key to getting people to talk

For most people, a smile shows that you are friendly and approachable.

Does anyone like talking to someone who has a scowl on their face? The answer is 'no' for most of us because scowls can be intimidating, thus making one unapproachable. A smile, on the other hand, helps you connect and makes people want to talk to you.

4. Say something that is mutually relevant to you both to get someone to talk

For example, you can tell someone in the check-out line how beautiful it is outside or how good the service is at the store you are shopping at. Comments like these, which are positive, can be a good way to get people to talk to you.

5. Listen to what they are saying when they are talking to you

When you listen the right way people will see you are interested in them and what they have to say. With this approach, not only do you make a connection with others, but you can also gather information you can use to help people to keep talking to you.

6. Use questions to get people to talk to you

Again, you can ask "Isn't this a beautiful day?". This example is a simple one, but the point is that questions beg a response. Most people when asked if it's a beautiful day will respond in some way.

By listening to their answers, you will also be able to think up some relevant questions to ask.

7. Let them know you want them to talk to you

If the other person isn't talking to you and you want them to, let them know of your desire for them to do so.

Usually, when a person isn't talking to you there is a reason why. Try to give this some acknowledgement in expressing your eagerness to get them to talk to you.

Learning how to get people to talk to you is not a huge problem, unless of course you just don't want people talking to you. And that's okay too! But just in case you might someday want someone to talk to you when they aren't doing so, you can use the above advice to help you get people to talk to you.

How to Get People to Tell the Truth

There is perhaps nothing more irritating, while in conversation with another person, than when you discover that they are not telling the truth.

Interestingly enough, people lie in a huge variety of situations, from the cheating partner, to the boss who wants to appear like they are taking care of business, to the child who did something wrong.

However, there are some strategies that you can use to get people to tell the truth to you.

1. Stay calm when you first discover someone is not telling you the truth

Most people do feel betrayed and become upset when they discover someone not telling them the truth. It's normal to feel this way. But the worst thing you can do in a situation like this is to lose control of yourself and your reactions, no matter how badly you want to correct it.

However, the best thing to do is to continue listening and make mental notes of what the other person is saying for future use.

2. Confront them about the truth at the right time

To get someone to tell the truth requires some strategy, especially involving timing. Moreover, when people are not telling the truth there is often a litter of small mistruths supporting the one they are telling you. It's these small mistruths that can help you focus on the truth that is missing from the person you are talking to.

When the opportunity presents itself, confront the individual about the mistruths you know. Point out the little mistruths you have heard, guiding the conversation to the truth you are seeking.

However, many people who don't speak the truth will defend their ground with rationalization, so that it at least makes sense to them and they can feel comfortable with themselves. Be prepared for this.

3. Gather supporting evidence

It is important to show the person who is not speaking the truth that you know they are lying. It's easier for a person to be untruthful if there isn't any evidence to the contrary.

The more facts and evidence you can present to them the more difficult it becomes for them to deny the truth. Most people, when faced with the evidence, will come clean with the truth.

4. Get the other person to look you in the eye when they are answering you

People's eyes often speak the truth, even when they don't want them to. If someone can't look you in the eyes when you ask them specific questions about their truthfulness it's a good indication that they are not being truthful with you.

One good way to break through their lies is to encourage them to look you in the eyes when they speak. This technique can prove very effective with trying to get the truth from a child, in particular.

5. Involve a third party to confront the person who is not telling the truth

This is not about ganging up on the person who is not telling the truth. But it is about bringing in a third party who is aware of the situation. Talk to that third party and recruit their assistance. Concerned third parties can be an invaluable help in getting the truth from someone.

6. Appreciate why people might lie

People usually lie out of fear of telling the truth to you. Therefore, you need to put their fears to rest, to some extent.

Tell them how you can work things through if the situation is B (what you suspect), rather than A (what they are telling you). Let them know that the worst case scenario is to lie, and that if you know the truth, you can work with them to resolve the situation.

How to get someone to tell the truth is a challenge. It requires you to listen, make note of discrepancies, and confront that person who is not telling the truth. Follow those tips to get people to tell the truth.

How to Get People to Trust You

The most valuable asset anyone can have, in interactions with others, is trust. Trust is the number one value between parties of any interaction. Even when first meeting someone we automatically begin to evaluate their trustworthiness.

Trust is an intrinsic part of human nature. It is part of our natural protection system and has been one of the most important foundations of all human connections since the beginning of time.

Therefore, if you want to develop good relationships with other people, it is very important that you know how to get people to trust you.

If you want to gain the trust of others there are some things you can do:

1. Get to know people well if you want them to trust you

People develop trust for others through familiarity and experience. The more you get to know someone the more they will trust you, and vice versa, unless you specifically break that trust.

Trust is the result of the reciprocal familiarity and experience with those that are around you and involved with your life on a regular basis.

You can't expect people to trust you from the start, but you need to work on being trustworthy from the beginning of a relationship. That way, you don't begin from a deficit of having already appeared untrustworthy. Once trust is broken, it is difficult to get it back.

2. Spend time with those you are interested in getting to know

The best way to build the trust that you want people to have in you is to be around the people you want to build a trust with. This of course goes hand in hand with getting to know people.

Courting is a good example of spending time to gain trust of another. As the relationship develops and grows the more trust that is given to each partner from the other

3. Be available to help those around you

A great way to help build trust is to think beyond ourselves when it comes to the needs of others. You might ask, "How can me helping others build trust?" The answer is this: "People will gain trust in you due to your positive behaviors and the help that you give to others with positive behavior."

4. Be honest with all those around you, even when that honesty might hurt

One of the strange things about honesty is that it can hurt in some situations. But when you are honest in all situations you will get respect which will translate into people trusting you. If you are dishonest with someone, word has a way of getting around to others and gaining trust from any of those people then becomes more difficult.

5. Be sincere in your intentions with everyone

The key to people believing your intentions is in your follow through. If you say "I will do that" then do it to the best of your abilities. If you can't do it for some reason then let the other person know.

Most of trust building is founded in your communications with others. Part of your communicating with others requires you to be sincere if you expect to gain the trust of those around you.

Getting people to trust you is totally your responsibility. By demonstrating trustworthy behaviors you will gain the trust of those around you. The flip side to the coin of trust is: "if you violate people's trust, it's a challenge to regain".

These are some simple methods to get people to trust you and avoid losing trust. Use these as a your starting point to get peoples trust.

How to Get People to Understand You

There will be times, with all the interactions you have on a daily basis, that someone is not going to understand you.

At work you may try to explain a procedure to a coworker; in a social situation, like a restaurant, it's important for wait staff to understand your order; and then, there is your private life where it's very important to you that those close to you, understand you.

There are numerous situations where you will want people to understand you.

Here are some thoughts about how to get people to understand you.

1. Be in control when explaining yourself

Don't let your emotions be the ruler, but the fuel of who you are. It's an awesome thing to have a great idea that you are passionate about, but if you let passion dominate your wisdom you will lose control of more than explaining yourself. If you want people to understand you relax, in the confidence of who you are, and explain yourself.

2. Speak with clarity as you explain yourself

If you want people to understand you, then you are responsible for speaking in such a way that they can understand you. This involves knowing what you want to say. Once you know what you want to say, practice it a few times before you present to your audience.

When you want to be understood, avoid using language that is unfamiliar to those to whom you are talking. If street language is what those you are talking to understand best then use that language so they may have a better chance of understanding what you are saying. And definitely don't use high class language because it could send a wrong message.

Similarly, if you are talking with a boss or other important person you won't want to use street language to elicit their understanding. You will run the risk of losing them as they are forced to ask, "what does that mean?"

Speak in a language that your particular audience can understand and be clear if you want others to understand what you are saying.

3. Appear that you want to be understood by those to whom you are talking

That means that you need to have confidence in what you be will saying. Confidence is about knowing what you're going to say before you say it and in knowing that what you are saying is correct and useful or interesting to your audience.

Practice can enhance your confidence.

Your body language will also tell others if you are sincere about being understood. For example, if you are running your fingers through your hair, while trying to explain something to someone, you are demonstrating nervousness and insecurity, neither of which help you to be understood.

4. Be reliably honest

This is essential if you want people to listen long enough to understand you. Some people consistently lie or fabricate stories and then wonder why they can't get any understanding when they really need it. It's because of their past unreliability and dishonesty. If you want people to understand you be reliable and honest.

5. Point out similarities between what you and others are saying

Similarities will help others understand you more clearly, and in addition, give more credence to what you are saying. When one sees commonalities it helps to make connections which in turn helps understanding. Thus, the more connections you can help someone make, the more understanding you can achieve.

If you want people to understand you than you must work at being understood.

These are some ways to get people to understand you. Put them into practice and you should get what you want: more understanding from the people to whom you are talking.

How to Get People to Want to Be around You

Getting people to be around you is really not all that difficult. Every human being is social by nature and we all want to be around other people.

Realistically, the problem of how to get people to want to be around you has more to do with you than it does others. For example, if you are pompous and arrogant few people are going to want to be around you because of your overbearing personality.

The first lesson is this: what attracts people to you, or causes them to avoid you, is your personality and attitude. The good news is that if you want people to be around you there are some points to bear in mind that can help you.

1. Accept and honor yourself

This idea may sound confusing on the surface. But it's not if you think about it. One of the best things you can do for yourself is to accept yourself as you are and honor that.

Acceptance and honor from others comes from our confidence in ourselves, because we accept ourselves, mixed with a healthy amount of humbleness and humility. People are attracted to this kind of balance because you are being 'real.'

2. Act naturally

This reflects confidence in oneself. When your inner feeling of acceptance mixes appropriately with your thought processes you will act naturally, like a human that is comfortable with themselves. When you project a comfortable feeling about yourself this helps others to feel comfortable with you, thus attracting them to you.

3. Don't make fun of others to make yourself feel better

It is fun, for example, at a party, to exchange friendly banter to get everyone loosened up and laughing. But to make fun of people because you think you are better than others will not attract people. It is distasteful to make fun of others in that way.

Avoid making fun of others for any reason. That's the best solution.

4. Don't focus on the mistakes of others

We all make them no matter how perfect we think we might be. If you have a need to focus on the mistakes of someone else turn that trait into something that helps them at a time they are receptive to your help. This technique has a way of building trust and friendship.

However, focusing on a mistake of another is a form of exploitation. It's an attack on the other person. When most people see you communicate in this manner with anyone they are already thinking about avoiding you.

If you have a problem with focusing on the mistakes of others then it is best you say nothing at all unless it is positive.

5. Think before you say anything

The words that come out of your mouth speaks volumes about the kind of person you are and what you believe in. Believe it or not everyone evaluates an initial interaction within the first few moments of that interaction. It's an instinct we all have.

Within those first few moments we are already deciding if it's a good connection or not.

Moreover, communication is not just about the words that come out of your mouth. There is a little more to it than that. We all watch each others' body language when we interact with each other. It's another instinct we have. We are more attentive to this sense within the first few interactions of meeting people, but as the familiarity grows we develop more trust and become less focused on personality traits.

These are some of the best ways how to get people to be around you. Apply these in your daily interactions and people will want to be around you.

How to Deal with Difficult People at Home

Dealing with difficult people at home can be more challenging than dealing with a difficult person outside of the home, where you can turn and walk away if you have to. You will usually have a closer bond with those people who live with or visit you than you do with people you work with or meet only outside the home.

Due to your bond with them, you need to use different strategies to deal with them.

1. Don't take it personally
When you deal with difficult people at home you can become susceptible to taking their difficult attitude personally, more so than you might when dealing with difficult people outside of the home. However, taking a difficult person's attitude personally will do nothing but make the situation all that more difficult.

When you think and feel it is personal you will be more apt to take a defensive position against the person who is causing you to feel that way. You then can become more concerned about protecting yourself than solving whatever problem the difficult person might be trying to convey.

2. Resist fighting back
Sometimes when you are dealing with a difficult person at home you may experience the desire to fight back and really give that person a piece of your mind or even worse.

Again, just like taking it personal, this will more than likely exasperate the situation and cause that person to become even more difficult, and could even cause them to feel justified in their behavior.

This is not to say you should become submissive and make way for the difficult person to say and do as they please. But you should remain calm and be intelligent in how you deal with a difficult person at home. The best thing to do is to put aside any emotions you might be feeling and become as objective as you can.

3. Avoid appeasement

Difficult people want to be right even when they know they're not. They also want to get their way even when they know they can't. This is part of the dynamics of difficult people. However, to appease a difficult one at home can be one of the worst things to do for both yourself and that difficult person.

When you appease a difficult person with anything other than solving a problem or reaching a mutual understanding you give that person permission to behave toward you any way they please and this is not healthy for you or the relationship with them. In fact, you will lose self respect and the respect of that difficult person.

4. Change them, not!

So many people who enter a relationship with a difficult person seem to think that they can change that person. No one can change another person. People change because that is what they know they need to do not because someone else thinks that's what the other needs to do.

Moreover, once you think and start acting like you can change difficult people at home they will more than likely rebel against those attempts. When a difficult person rebels you then can become their direct target and find them blaming you for their attitude.

5. Set the expectations

There may be times that someone who is visiting your home becomes difficult to deal with. When this happens, immediately let them know whose home they are in and warn them that you won't put up with their difficult behavior.

If this doesn't cause them to change their attitude then ask them to leave.

These tips are not the only ones there are for dealing with difficult people at home, but they are the best ones to preserve yourself as a person and let that difficult person know that you are not a doormat upon which they can impose any bad behavior they choose.

How to Deal with Difficult People at Work

Wherever you work, you are likely to meet difficult people. It could be coworkers, bosses or customers with whom you have to deal. Thankfully, depending on who they are and how they behave, you can develop strategies to deal with difficult people at work.

1. Rise above it

Largely, your response to other people is triggered by your own self esteem and how you feel about yourself. You are in charge of that.

It is much easier to deal with difficult people at work if there are a lot of people. That way, you have allies, also treated badly by that person, who can help you deal with them.

But what about if you are the only person dealing with that difficult one? Then you have to fall back on your own self confidence. Be sure you are doing your job properly and you are treating people well, then you can tell yourself it is the difficult person's problem, not yours and you can forget about it to a large extent.

2. Develop good relationships

Develop good, positive relationships with everyone you work with. Do your job well, but accept and ask for help when necessary.

Appreciate those you work with and the job that they do. If you respect other people at work they are more likely to respect you and be less difficult with you.

3. Give effective feedback

If someone is being difficult at work, often, you will need to do something about that. You may have to give them some feedback. The way you do that is important if it is to be effective.

First, ask if it's okay to give the person an opinion and if it's a good time. It is always better to talk to them when they want to listen to you. Give them a heads up so that if you have to tell them something that may be difficult for them to hear, tell them that so they can prepare for it.

Be straightforward and simple. Tell the person the issue and the impact it is having on other people. Let them know the positive impact that behaving differently would have on people. That will help them see a reason to change.

Also, talk with them about ways they could change their behavior. They may not see these ways for themselves, especially at first.

4. Dealing with negativity in a coworker

We all know people who just love to complain and see the darker side of things, don't we? But that kind of negativity can drag you down and get you depressed if you let it. Instead, be proactive.

The first thing to do, although you may not feel like it, is to listen to the negative comments. Then you can decide if they are justified. They might be: in which case, you have something to work on and improve.

If they are unjustified as far as you are concerned, then just a listening ear may be all the other person needs.

You could try sympathy, saying "I can see how that would be really bad." Sometimes that can shock the negative person into thinking things really aren't that bad after all!

5. Dealing with conflict

Often, people are afraid of conflict and that makes it difficult to deal with, especially when it makes you doubt yourself. If a conflict flares up, try to remain calm. If necessary, say that you need some time to think and arrange a time when you can talk together after you have calmed down.

Plan what resolution you want. Work out the points on which you must stand firm due to your beliefs and self respect, and those on which you can compromise to reach agreement.

These steps should help you deal with difficult people at work no matter what issues you have to tackle with them.

How to Deal with Difficult People on the Phone

Often, you will have to deal with difficult people on the phone because it is your job to do so. Knowing how to deal with them effectively entails understanding about boundaries: yours and theirs.

1. Keep calm
You will only inflame the situation further if you get angry and that won't help anyone. You are safe on the end of a telephone line so you should not feel threatened or get defensive.

2. Listen
Often, people are difficult on the telephone because they don't know how to phrase their points well or because they are unsure about the validity of what they are asking you to do.
You will only know what you can do for the other person if you listen to them actively and check that you have understood what they are saying. Listening will also allow the other person to vent their emotions and get it out of their system.
You must listen particularly carefully on the phone to discern meaning because you will not be picking up any nonverbal cues which normally help you understand meaning.

3. Allow people to say what they need to
Don't interrupt them. Remember they are on the other end of the phone and therefore not posing a direct threat to you. Therefore, you should not have a problem in letting them vent.
If you try to cut them off or appear not to be listening, you will only frustrate them further and make constructive communication more difficult.

4. Retain your integrity
No matter how abusive or difficult the person on the other end of the phone conversation gets, do not sink to that level. State how you would like to help them but that insulting you and being disrespectful will not be tolerated.

5. Be empathic

Try to put yourself in the shoes of the other person and look at it from their point of view. Recognize their feelings and let them know you can understand how they feel the way they do. However, do not patronize them or pretend to feel the same way.

6. Ask questions

To be truly empathic, you need to understand the person and the situation in which they find themselves. This is why you need to ask questions, to ensure that you really do understand the situation.

Often you might think someone is being difficult on the phone purely because you don't understand the problem.

7. Seek a solution

Once you understand the situation, you should try to move toward a solution. Never promise to fix a problem, because that may not be possible. However, you can say that you will do your best to get a solution for them.

Often, if they believe you will do what you can to help, a difficult person's anger and stubbornness can be diffused.

8. Apologize if appropriate

Sometimes, you will have made a mistake that will have rightfully annoyed the other person. If you can genuinely say sorry, do so and it will help a lot in making them behave in a less difficult manner towards you.

9. Get approval for your solution

A solution is only any good if the other person is satisfied with the outcome. Therefore, do not impose a solution. Try get them to agree to it.

10. End the call if you want to

You can always put down the phone. Don't just slam it down, of course. Just explain that you have done what you can and that is where your responsibility ends. It's not ideal, but it may be your best and only option in the end.

So, even though you don't have nonverbal cues to pick up on, you can learn how to deal with difficult people on the phone. Just keep calm, and be clear about what your limits and responsibilities are.

How to Deal with Difficult People in Life

The trick in learning how to deal with difficult people in life lies in the acceptance that you can't control their behavior but you can control your own.

1. Get the problem in perspective

When you think that someone is impossible, what that means is that they really annoy you. They may annoy you a lot, but the situation is not impossible to deal with. Once you appreciate that, you can begin to get the problem in perspective.

Realizing that you have some power over the situation and your reactions to it can often calm you down.

2. How do they annoy you?

If you can rationalize what it is that annoys you about the person you find difficult to handle, you can begin to deal with it. Given some time and space to think, you will be able to think about what is annoying you, without feeling so emotionally upset about it.

3. Talk to the person

You can't hope to be able to get on better with someone you find impossible without talking to them. But that talk needs to wait until you can be calm about it.

When you feel calm, talk to the person privately or maybe with a neutral third person there. Let them know, calmly and clearly, what it is that they are doing that annoys you. Do not get angry and do not keep going on about the point.

Just tell them what upsets you and how it makes you feel. For instance: "It makes me feel useless when you ask me to do something but then just take over and do it yourself".

4. Listen

Once you have had your say about what you find difficult to deal with in the other person, give them the right to reply. The only way to really deal with impossible people constructively is to understand their point of view.

Therefore, you need to listen respectfully to how they view the situation. This can be quite enlightening if you really listen, showing you the way forward in how to deal with them.

5. Discuss a compromise

Hopefully, if you have had a calm, rational time where you have stated what annoys you, and you have listened to what the other person has to say on the matter, you will be able to see a way forward. Try to find a solution which gives you both respect and which accepts something of what you both want.

6. See the good in everyone

If you approach your interactions calmly and in good humor, everyone has good points to their character, no matter how impossible they may seem at first. Acknowledging a person's good points may help them become less impossible as they ease off if they feel appreciated.

For instance, a person may seem impossibly domineering, but this may be motivated by their own insecurities. So, you could say to them, "I think it's great how well organized you are with this party; I wonder how I could help?"

This may give them a hint that they have been somewhat domineering. Also, it shows them that you appreciate what they are doing and that may boost their confidence enough to make them let go of the reins a little and allow you to participate.

7. Consider removing the person from your life

You may have to cut the impossible person out of your life. If they are not important to you, you may decide that they are not worth the effort to reach an understanding. However, you may miss out on something very valuable this way.

So, before you decide to cut someone out of your life, do all you can to learn how to deal with impossible people. You will be a stronger, happier person for it, and you will perhaps learn a lot about yourself and other people.

How to Deal with Difficult Family Members

Learning how to deal with difficult family members can be one of the most challenging of all relationships. With outgrown or toxic friendships you can close the door and move on with your life.

You can't do that so easily with family members who are critical, negative, or controlling because they are family, flesh and blood. You can't just turn, walk away, and forget about difficult family members because they will always be there in your midst.

So what can you do? Here are a few tips on how to deal with difficult family members.

1. Change you, not them

Some people think that, with enough effort and time, they can change the behavior of a difficult person. However, to think you can change somebody is delusional thinking because you cannot change anyone except yourself. You are a human being, not a god.

So how do you change yourself so you can more effectively deal with difficult family members?

First, change how you see the difficult family member through understanding their behavior. This understanding can be gained by talking to other family members to find out the reasons why this person is the way he is.

And second, change how you react to that difficult family member.

If that person is pushing your buttons don't give them the satisfaction of provoking you, instead respond by saying something positive, maybe a compliment, or possibly even turning your hot button into a joke of some sort.

The point is to side step the difficult person's negativity.

2. Employ compassion

Using compassion to deal with a difficult family member is not the easiest thing in the world to do. Honestly, it can seem like it's nearly impossible especially if you have some resentment regarding the difficult family member's behavior.

However, you would probably have compassion if that difficult person was the member of someone else's family and you did not have to deal with them so much. That being the case, shouldn't that compassion be extended to a difficult person in your family?

3. Check yourself

Sometimes a difficult family member will mirror something that is also in you. Often we see behaviors in others that we don't like and often it is a behavior we don't like about ourselves.

At these times it's so easy for you to focus on the difficult person to avoid addressing that behavior in yourself. But this tactic does no one any good, especially you because you deny yourself the opportunity of change and growth.

The next time you are dealing with a difficult family member look at yourself first before examining them. And if you fix you, it could make the relationship much more pleasant, and if it doesn't, at least it will make you a better person.

4. Be true and sincere

In the context of dealing with a difficult family member, being true and sincere means not compromising your beliefs and feelings.

Maybe you did something for the difficult family member that you really didn't want to do. This will cause you regret and guilt, and then resentment toward the person you did it for.

This resentment will then taint your perception of that person and your relationship with them with negativity. That would be a shame as it will prevent you seeing the good aspects of the relationship.

So, the next time someone asks you to do something that you don't want to do be honest with sincerity and let them know the truth.

The secret to dealing with difficult family members is to not try to change them, but change yourself in how you perceive them and how you react to that perception.

How to Deal with Angry People

Angry people are all around us and in our everyday lives. We come across angry people at work, while out in public places, and even at home. Sometimes a person is directly angry at us because of something we may have done or not done. At other times we are not the cause of a person's anger but become the target of it.

Regardless if we are the cause of it or not we still find ourselves having to deal with it. What follows are some techniques to help you to deal with angry people.

1. Kill anger with kindness

One of the best ways of dealing with an angry person is not to take it personally and be attentive to them, using kindness as you are talking to them. More times than not, words and acts of kindness heal anger like ointment on an open wound.

If the angry person is angry at you for something find out what it is and apologize for the error of judgement in a genuine and sincere manner. But above all don't indulge in the behavior. That is, don't let their anger make you angry.

If you do it will be like throwing fuel on a burning flame and no one benefits when that happens.

2. Limit the interaction

Some angry people look for a good fight sometimes. If you know an angry person who seems to be looking for a fight distance yourself from them quickly, especially if there is any mind altering substances involved.

Do not even try to rationalize with an angry person who is not sober. You will not win in defeating the anger of an intoxicated person and your attempts will only cause their anger to escalate.

3. Set boundaries

Set boundaries, especially concerning respect. However, be aware that if you want an angry person to respect you then you must first respect yourself.

Allowing people to walk all over you translates into a lack of self-respect and angry people are perceptive about who they choose as their target to lash out at.

If the angry person is a family member or friend let them know immediately that you will not tolerate being used as their whipping post. Grab onto your self-respect and put your foot down firmly against misdirected anger.

4. Separate yourself

Anger is a natural human emotion that we all experience from time to time. For example, a wife will become angry at her husband for not listening to her when she politely asked him to pick up a few things from the grocery store on his way home from work.

In this situation her anger would be justified because she had expected him to do something she asked of him.

However, if you have a family member or friend who is consistently behaving angrily, no matter what you do or don't do, then it may be wise to separate yourself from that person permanently, or at least until they can get some help and a grip on their behavior.

Allowing yourself to remain around negative and hostile people will only harm you. Angry and negative people do nothing but create angry and negative situations for themselves and the people around them.

How you deal with angry people will largely depend on your relationship with them. You can walk away from an angry person you ran into at the grocery store. It becomes a little more complicated when dealing with an angry family member or friend. The most point, however, is to have self-respect and not let angry people use you as their target for unwarranted anger.

How to Deal with Ignorant People

A person becomes ignorant when they think, they are educated when they're not, know something when they don't, or are more aware than others. And so these people can cause us frustration and irritate us.

Ignorance is defined by Webster's Dictionary as "a lack of knowledge, education, or awareness". Now, not being aware, educated, or knowledgeable is not a negative thing in itself. It simply implies that a person doesn't know or isn't aware of something.

For example, a computer geek may be knowledgeable about computers but doesn't know a thing about cars or aware that if he doesn't put water in the radiator the engine could overheat and become damaged.

What is more damaging is when one is ignorant in such a way that they think they know more than others and refuse to listen to others' viewpoints.

Here are some tips on how to deal with ignorant people.

1. Ignore them

Ignorant people and rude people are similar in the sense that they both need attention. The rude person is invasive to get attention while the ignorant person is a know-it-all. The ignorant person wants to impress people with his mental abilities. However, both the ignorant person and the rude person can be equally annoying.

But you can deal with the ignorant person just like you would the rude person. That is, ignore them. Ignoring the ignorant person is perhaps the best way to deal with them; they need the attention of others to make them feel good about what they think they know.

2. Be kind

Be kind to someone who irritates you? This sounds difficult and perhaps it is. But if you understand that ignorant people are not well informed and not necessarily bad, then you can access empathy for them.

Many ignorant people learned to talk about or say things they know nothing about. They also have learned to give opinions without knowing all the facts.

You can often deal with ignorant people by just gently educating them about the situation. Being kind not only helps you down the road, but it also has the potential of placing you in a good position with the ignorant person.

3. Speak to the person

Some ignorant people can be hard headed about their behavior, primarily because they may have a deep need to protect their ego from correction. This type of ignorant person can be a little more difficult to deal with. However, in some instances you can deal with them by taking them aside, away from distractions, and explain how their behavior is damaging their reputations.

This could be especially effective for employers to use with ignorant employees that just don't seem to get it otherwise. There is little that could disrupt morale and production more than an ignorant person that is talking work related issues that they really don't totally understand, for example, talking about who will be laid-off when they are not part of management and in the know.

4. Have patience

Many ignorant people don't realize that they don't know everything involved in a particular situation, but instead assume that they do with the little information that have. They are presumptuous too. But, again, this doesn't make them bad people.

One of the most effective tools you can use in dealing with ignorant people is patience. Using patience helps you remain calm whenever interacting with ignorant people and helps them to slow down a bit and think it through before talking.

How to deal with ignorant people requires time and patience more than anything else. It also requires you to gently educate the ignorant person so that they can see the whole of a situation before they conclude that they know what it's all about.

How to Deal with Obnoxious People

Obnoxious people can be extremely annoying, especially loud boisterous ones. You know the ones we're talking about. They come into a room with flamboyance and a loud voice to signal to all that they have arrived.

Obnoxious people also think that they're better than everyone else and will speak louder than the average person about your faults so other people can hear it.

Or how about the one that makes you a target of their offbeat jokes?

As you are quite well aware, obnoxious people can be an embarrassment to be around. However, an obnoxious person isn't a bad person. For many, they have been obnoxious for so long they don't even realize that they're being obnoxious.

Fortunately for them there are some things you can do to help. Here are three ways to deal with obnoxious people.

1. Face to face communication

It's important for the obnoxious person, if they are to become aware of their obnoxious behavior, for you meet with them face to face. You should also make this meeting only between the obnoxious person and yourself.

It's not helpful if other parties are present because then the obnoxious person may feel like they are being ganged up on. And this will only put them on the defensive. When that happens they will not listen and will more than likely become aggressively boisterous and obnoxious. The result of that will be that you will never be given that opportunity again.

With that in mind, schedule a meeting with the obnoxious person at a location that is comfortable and where there will be no interruptions.

2. Be prepared

Before the scheduled meeting it would help both the obnoxious person and yourself if you were to make a list of points that you would like to cover when you are talking to each other. This list should consist of not only the things about the obnoxious person that bother you, but also the reasons and the specific situations in which the obnoxious person was obnoxious.

A list of points will help you keep the meeting focused so that the obnoxious person and you can get the most out of it. Without a list the meeting has the potential to wander aimlessly around and not accomplish anything.

3. Explain your position

Start the meeting by explaining why you want to talk to the obnoxious person. As you explain the reasons why to them be sure to maintain eye contact.

Eye contact is especially important whenever explaining how and why the obnoxious person makes you feel the way you do. Eye contact sends the message that you are sincere about what you are saying to the other person. If you don't maintain eye contact the obnoxious person will not take you seriously.

After you explain why you arranged the meeting with the obnoxious person you can begin discussing the points you wrote down on your list.

As you are discussing these points don't talk to the obnoxious person in a condescending manner, but instead speak to them as if you are their equal, which you are if you think about. The obnoxious person is a human being just like you, but just needs a little help to become aware of their behavior.

Also, be prepared and keep yourself open to listening to the obnoxious person's responses. Listening makes a discussion a two way street and encourages the other's participation.

You can learn how to deal with obnoxious people in a humanistic way. Remember, many obnoxious people don't realize they are obnoxious because they are just being themselves, behaving in a way they have for many years. If you are sincere and patient you just might win the obnoxious person over to changing their behavior.

How to Deal with Passive Aggressive People

Passive aggressive behavior may include sulking and sullenness; consistently being late, or not completing tasks; making excuses or blaming others for poor performance; procrastination; fear of intimacy and a lack of trust in people; making sarcastic or hurtful comments and generally behaving like a victim.

Passive aggressive behavior stems from a person feeling powerless and inferior, and using their behavior as a means of controlling or punishing others.

An assertive approach is recommended in dealing with passive aggressive people.

1. Find out as much as you can about passive aggressive behavior from books, leaflets and websites, or consult a professional in personality disorders.

2. Learn to emotionally detach yourself from your loved one's dysfunctional attitudes.

You neither have to agree with them, nor get into constant fights: just walk out of the room.

Don't go round and round the same old conversations about their behavior; your words will simply go unheard.

3. Do not allow your loved one to control you or isolate you. They will be tempted to break down your personal barriers; to cut you off from friends and other family members; to tell you where you can go, and who you are permitted to see.

If you don't resist, you will find yourself being drawn into their world, and gradually lose yourself. You will forfeit your self esteem and lose sight of reality.

You need to establish firm boundaries against this kind of controlling behavior, and ensure that you maintain your life outside the relationship, seeing friends, pursuing leisure interests etc.

4. You need to realize that you can neither control the other persons behavior, nor 'fix' them. You are not responsible for them, or for their behavior. You must also realize that you cannot and should not even try to meet all of your loved ones needs.

Don't devote your whole life to them: you are just as important, and have to look out for your own needs. This will make you feel stronger and healthier, and better able to cope.

5. People close to those with passive aggressive behavior should not simply ignore it, or let the other person get away with their bad behavior by adopting a 'forgive and forget' attitude towards it; otherwise they will never learn from their mistakes, and will continue along their self-destructive road.

This form of 'enabling' often results in short-term gains leading to long-term loss, since condoning your loved ones behavior will often cause it to escalate.

6. Get support from other people. Talking through your problems can make them seem less overwhelming and if you don't talk about things, resentment can build up like poison in your soul.

Good friends can help: you can trust them, and the warmth of their friendship will help to sustain you. It might also help to talk to a therapist or counselor who understands the difficulties of being in a relationship with someone who has a personality disorder.

7. As a final option, if your loved one's abuse and behavior are beginning to ruin your life, and you have finally realized that they are never going to change, you might have to make the difficult and painful decision to withdraw from the relationship and go 'no contact'.

Never try to use this as a bluff to try to make your loved one change, though, as it won't ever work. If you leave, you have to mean it: that you have given up all hope that they will ever get better if you only stand by them for long enough. It doesn't mean that you have ceased to love them.

If you do leave, you are bound to suffer a form of bereavement; you will feel guilt, and probably some fear. Allow yourself time to grieve, and then start to rediscover yourself. Don't rush into another relationship until you have fully recovered, and don't just start another relationship that will follow the same pattern; look for someone who will be good for you.

Living with a passive aggressive person can be like constantly trying to scale a mountain, and one gradually becomes weaker and more frustrated when unable to reach the summit. By taking a proactive approach to understanding and dealing with a loved one's behavior, you can begin to take your first steps to taking back control of your life.

How to Deal with Rude People

Aren't rude people so annoying? Unfortunately, rude people are everywhere. We run into rude people on the job, at the grocery store, in restaurants, and in practically any other place where people come together. Yes, we even run into rude people at home.

But dealing with rude people can be a bit tricky because they generally arouse a degree of irritation and anger within us so we are less likely to think of logical ways to deal with the situation.

Here are a few ideas on how to deal with rude people.

1. Rude people want attention

One reason rude people are the way they are is because they want attention and being rude is the only way they think they can get it. So don't give them the attention they are seeking.

When a rude person doesn't get the attention they want and expect they quickly lose impetus because their attempt at making you mad has failed. When they don't get your attention it irritates them.

2. Don't respond, shake it off

Not responding to a rude person goes beyond not talking to them. It also involves body language responses as well, such as not even looking at them.

Again, people who are rude want attention and they are very keen on even the subtlest responses and look for them whenever they don't get a verbal response. If they see the slightest irritation in your body language they will continue being rude until they push you into responding.

The best strategy is to completely ignore them, shake off any negative emotions that may be aroused, and move on.

3. Who is right doesn't matter

Some rude people will blatantly say or ask you something that is really none of their business. Rude people are naturally intrusive about other people's business and even if you were to satisfy their curiosity they would only seek more.

It wouldn't cause them to be nicer to you and it wouldn't make a difference in your life one way or the other. It will save you a great deal of time and much aggravation if you just ignore them.

4. Rude to one, rude to all

If a rude person is rude to someone they will be rude to you too. Rude people are generally indiscriminate about who they are rude to because being rude is a part of their personality. They don't care how they make anyone else feel, but themselves.

It's all about them and nobody else. When a rude person makes someone feel bad they get some gratification from it and this feeds their rude behavior.

5. Rude people in the work place

Rude people in the work place are on a mission other than just working. They want to make coworkers feel inferior and that they are owed something, However, confronting rude coworkers can be a bit tricky; if you challenge them too aggressively they could turn the tables on you and you may find yourself in your bosses office trying to explain the situation and you don't want that.

The best thing to do is to try to put them in their place diplomatically and if that doesn't work do it is best just to ignore them. If the behavior persists you may want to consider letting your supervisor know so that they can intervene.

Dealing with rude people can be tricky business depending on the environment in which the rude person is being rude. But the easiest way to deal with them is to just ignore and not give them the satisfaction of eliciting a response from you.

How to Deal with Selfish People

All selfish people are self-centered and don't care about anyone else but themselves which can mean it is difficult to know how to deal with selfish people. Everything has revolved around them for so long that they don't even realize they are destroying their relationships with their friends or loved ones.

But if we want to keep them around, especially the ones close to us, we have to learn how to deal with them. Their never ending story about themselves can be very annoying to some people, and the best thing to do is change the subject and move on.

However, there are some more ways to help us deal with selfish people. Here are some good ways to handle these difficult individuals.

1. Have patience

If this person is troubled the best way to deal with their selfishness is to try to bring them out of their negative frame of mind. For example, you can probably ask them why they have been rude and critical of others.

You can mention that nobody is perfect and that they might be able to open up to you and explain what is causing them to behave this way so you can understand them better. The best way is to be patient with them.

You may be able to help them feel better about themselves and about others.

2. Be sensitive

You also have to consider that someone who is rude and selfish may have some personal problems and feel that they just can't share what is going on in their lives. They are rude because they do not want to get close to people and do not want to feel hurt by others.

Try to be sensitive and be understanding about their past and perhaps they will see their own self-interest and become less critical of others. In other words, show that you are trying to help them.

3. Limit your interaction

If nothing else works you may have to limit your interactions with the selfish person while still keeping them in your life. There are a few strategies that have been successful dealing with selfish people.

For example, be kind, and stay cool. They know that they're difficult and won't respect you if you pretend they aren't. If you have a good sense of humor, use it. Everyone loves to laugh. But keep the interaction short and sweet until you see some change.

4. Set boundaries

It would be easier to give some guidance than it is to set boundaries, but you may have to draw the line if the relationship is damaging to you. It may be your only choice if you must stay involved with this person.

Remind them of the situations that were painful for you and ask why they act the way they do. And don't accept excuses for their behavior because excuses are a way to avoid responsibility. You either build relationships through talking it out or you have to set boundaries if talking doesn't solve the problem.

Above all, don't judge them.

5. Distance yourself

Don't let selfish people mistreat you. The best way is to simply stop cooperating with their mistreatment. Also, you don't want to repeat this kind of behavior. That is why distancing yourself may be wise.

The reason they are mistreating people is because it is rewarding for them in some way. So the answer is to stop cooperating and separate yourself from them.

Selfish people choose to be negative and pursue behavior that hurts others so they can feel better about themselves. Ultimately, surrounding yourselves with negative people can arouse negativity in you. It's important to make good decisions about who you associate with.

How to Deal with Unreasonable People

From prickly in-laws to difficult coworkers, we have all found ourselves trying, and usually failing to successfully deal with unreasonable people. There are several strategies however that you can employ to turn a frustrating, embarrassing situation into a more positive experience.

1. Stay calm

This sounds both simple and deceptively easy, but it is critical to emerging unscathed.

Unreasonable people are not interested in facts, your opinion, or who is right. They only want to provoke you into responding with the same amount of ire and negativity that they feel.

Remember that there is one small pearl of truth in all of their bombast and focus on that.

2. Acknowledge their feelings

By pinpointing their argument, and acknowledging their anger, you can redirect the focus back to their behavior without responding in kind.

For example; "Yes, politicians are usually dishonest, and you sound very angry about this" is more constructive than "I happened to vote for X because he is smart and talented, not because he lied on his College application".

3. See it as their problem

Always remember that such unreasonable people are often projecting their own faults and anger onto you. It is literally their problem, not yours. They will hurl unreasonable anger at you irrespective of your response.

It is difficult to remember not to retort defensively, and focus on what the real issue is. This is crucial in maintaining your own equilibrium while trying to defuse the situation.

Try to think of their ire as a box that they are thrusting at you. If you don't take it, they are left holding it.

4. Don't try to win a pointless argument

It is also crucial to not get caught in the 'lose or win' mentality. You cannot 'win' this confrontation with logic, facts, personal opinions, or even a signed testimony from the Pope! Like the computer in the movie War Games learned; "The only winning move is not to play."

You can acknowledge their anger and facts but you will never change them.

5. Be civil even if others are not

Try not to treat them with the same disregard for civility and rationality they are showing you. It will be a triumph of self control that many still have not fully mastered, yet still strive to attain!

By showing them the level of respect that you wish to be treated with, you also can move the argument back into the realm of positivity. But when you argue on their level, or at their volume, they will see this as winning, and strive to continue the conflict.

Capricious and arbitrary coworkers can be dealt with using these tactics, but remember that this behavior is unprofessional and intolerable in the office environment.

Any confrontations witnessed by coworkers will automatically win the sympathy and respect of the crowd if you can keep your cool and deflect.

If the unreasonable anger comes from your boss, here are a few tools to work with:

6. Request needed resources

When he demands the impossible from you, rather than tell him how futile it is, request what you need to accomplish the task.

This keeps the focus on what he wants done, and reminds him of what is truly involved to achieve it.

7. Request a mediator

If your supervisor persists in abusive or pointless arguing with you, you are well within your rights to request a mediator of some sort. Asking for another supervisor's presence will help everyone focus on what really needs to happen, rather than permitting your boss to rail at you.

In all confrontations with unreasonable people, your crucial focus should be to remember that you are not the deluded person here! You will never change the world with one successfully defused senseless argument, but you can emerge with your own sanity and dignity intact.

How to Deal with Verbal Abuse

Human beings demonstrate abuse of another in many different ways, from a grimace every time we are near someone we don't like to full blown physical attacks. Disrespecting people by not making way for them or making rude comments about them impeding your way is a subtle form of abuse, but the nonetheless it's just that: abuse.

However, one of the most painfully penetrating, of the long list of abuses, is verbal abuse.

So, how do we deal with verbal abuse? It's not easy, but here's a short list of how to deal with verbal abuse.

1. Love yourself

First things first. The best shield of protection against verbal abuse is to love yourself. If you have good self esteem, you will be less concerned by any verbal abuse from other people, because you will realize that whatever they say does not change who you are.

That means to know in your heart and mind that you are an important person and no matter what anyone says to you or about you does not alter who you are. This understanding and belief in yourself is the best defense against personalizing verbal abuse and letting it damage you.

2. Zero tolerance

Just think about it, if more people loved themselves there would be less tolerance for verbal abuse from us all. However, individually speaking we each must have zero tolerance for verbal abuse from those we interact with.

If nobody tolerates this bad behavior, then those who are more apt to give out verbal abuse will realize that it is pointless.

When somebody starts abusing you, you must put your foot down and put a stop to it. Physically walk away if you have to. You are not doing anyone any good (including the abuser) if you accept verbal abuse.

3. Let them know you will not tolerate abuse

To reinforce your zero tolerance of verbal abuse you must let the verbal abuser know how much their words hurt you and that you will not accept being spoken to like that. Be firm and persistent about it. Do not get upset or angry. Just calmly state that you will not tolerate being spoken to in that way.

Do not ask the person who is abusing you how they would like it done to them because it would be ignored. Instead, be straightforward and establish your boundaries of acceptable behavior.

4. Talk to a third party

Many people have family members who can't control their fury. They then speak to their loved ones with hatred and disrespect, not only once or twice, but constantly and consistently.

These types of situations, especially if they have been long term, require you to seek a third party of some sort, like a counselor. That will at least give you the opportunity to talk about it. From that you will get support.

Third parties can be other family members, friends, counsellors or religious advisers, too. The important point when dealing with a habitual abusive person is for you to get help.

5. Remove yourself from the situation

Whenever a family member becomes verbally abusive our natural instinct is to react and defend ourselves. Defending ourselves involves our zero tolerance attitude, but in no way should we become abusive ourselves.

Look at it logically. What's the point? If you reciprocate verbal abuse with verbal abuse it will only make the other person angrier. Moreover, an abusive exchange can quickly become something physical and that won't help anyone.

No one has the right to abuse another human being. It's unacceptable behavior and now you have some strategies for dealing with verbal abuse that can help you to better handle these aggressive people.

How to Be Less Awkward around People

Believe it or not most people feel awkward around other people at one time or another. There are so many things that can cause any one of us to experience this feeling. And that's exactly what awkwardness is: a feeling.

You may think you are awkward because you spilled that drink down the front of your shirt or tripped over your untied shoelace, but that may not be how others perceive you.

This brings us to the most important point of how to be less awkward around other people.

1. Stop thinking of yourself as being awkward

Instead think confidently of yourself and when that drink does dribble down your shirt have fun with it by saying something like "there must be a hole in my lip." Reacting to a blunder by laughing at yourself can turn an embarrassing, awkward moment into a conversational icebreaker.

2. Assume rapport

Assuming rapport is about thinking how good a meeting or conversation will go rather than thinking of any negative possibilities. Assuming rapport will help you to relax and not worry so much about how you might fail and instead pay more attention to just having a conversation.

To assume rapport, approach the interaction like you would if you were going to talk to a good friend.

3. First impressions

Having a good mental attitude from the beginning of an interaction will result in you making a good first impression on people. Regardless of how awkward you might feel inside, smile when first meeting someone and then slowly ease yourself into talking with them. That is, listen carefully to find out what the other person's interests are.

Also, make short statements to ease yourself into further dialog. An awkward person should never just start rambling about anything under the sun because this will only worsen the awkward feeling and maybe even cause you to feel like you are stupid, neither of which will help you to be less awkward around people.

4. Be yourself

When you are around friends you generally don't worry about what to say next, but usually live in the moment, letting the interaction take on a life of its own. This is the moment when you are relaxed and yourself.

This simple idea can be applied as a strategy to help you be less awkward around people. Moreover, when you are being yourself you are more apt to enjoy any interaction that you might become involved with. Also, think of each interaction as an adventure of discovery because that is exactly what it is and not a means to expose you as being an awkward individual.

Remember, being awkward is a mindset, a thought process, but it's not something you are.

5. Have confidence

Being yourself entails having confidence in yourself and your abilities. People who think they are awkward lack confidence in themselves so much that they think people think of them like they think of themselves.

Does it really matter what other people think about you? No. So why should you focus on what people might think? It's vanity if you do.

Instead, focus on the fact that you are a human being just like everyone else, each with their own idiosyncrasies as well as desirable qualities.

Being less awkward around people is more about your thinking than it is anything else. Everyone has made silly blunders in their interactions with others at one time or other. Read the newspapers and see that even important and famous personalities can sometimes be awkward. But this doesn't stop them from being who they are or cause them to develop a complex about interacting with others. It should not affect you this way, either.

How to Talk without Arguing

Talking to another person without arguing is not an impossible feat. Talking without arguing is strictly an issue of self control.

Look to many of the worlds leaders. Without a doubt world leaders become angry while negotiating with each other. Although there are disagreements among them they talk to each other and control themselves so they do not argue, even though they probably want to.

These leaders have the same feelings the rest of us have, but a high level of self control. This is the key to talking without arguing.

Here are some tips to help you have self control and how to talk without arguing:

1. Stay focused on the key issues

Nothing can turn a disagreement into an argument faster than losing focus on the issues. Digressions, transgressions, accusations or anything else that detracts from what either of you are saying will result in an argument.

If you, or the person you are talking to, lose focus, immediately bring the discussion back to the original disagreement. If that doesn't work then agree to end the conversation before it becomes an argument.

2. Control your tongue

Even subtle insults couched in a statement can turn a productive conversation into an argument. And using profanity will only get it in return, thus escalating the discussion into an argument. You can usually avoid an argument by watching how you are talking to the other person. Again, use self control.

3. When you get too angry, step away

Here too it's about self control, but more importantly being able to identify when it's time to change the subject or totally remove yourself from the conversation. You will know your body signals that indicate arising anger and when you sense that kind of arousal that's the time that you need to remove yourself from the situation.

4. Remember that you're not always right

Many conversations turn into arguments because someone has to be right. Don't think that because you are right about some things it means you're right about everything. If you know everything then what is your purpose here amongst us human beings? To lead us? Good leaders make mistakes too.

5. Stop with the excuses

A conversation can blast off into an argument when the people involved start making excuses for themselves.

Some people will talk to you about an unacceptable behavior, for example. By making an excuse for it you have already placed yourself in a defensive position. If the one who is talking to you pushes on that position it could ignite an argument.

The best thing to do is not make excuses and avoid complicating the conversation.

6. Don't tell lies or fabricate a story

There almost nothing worse in a conversation than to lie or make up stories. Practically every person, even criminals, doesn't like being lied to and it's a guaranteed argument starter when the lie is discovered.

So, save yourself the grief of a heated argument and be truthful and honest.

7. Give respect and you could prevent an argument

Some people can become disrespectful toward the person they are talking to. For example, it's disrespectful for a man to eye a woman up and down while he's talking to her. This will most certainly make her feel uncomfortable and that could change a friendly meeting into an argument.

Watch that your body language and words are not sending a disrespectful message.

You can talk to other people on some quite difficult topics without arguing, but it does take self awareness and self control to keep a constructive conversation from spiraling downward into an argument. The above tips when combined can help you to talk without arguing.

How to Talk with Confidence

Having confidence in yourself can make a world of difference in relating to the outside world. If you fear what is out there you won't accomplish much toward your reason for being here. Each of us has a purpose, whatever that purpose might be. And we all have to discover it for ourselves. But in that discovery you will notice your confidence growing.

We all have varying degrees of confidence, and, it can change from challenge to challenge. For example, there are large numbers of people who don't have the confidence to talk to people. They are easy to identify because they have that look of "I want to say something, but I'm scared" on their faces.

These people listen attentively and are interested in the discussion, but may feel that their contribution will get laughed at. If you are one of those people who doesn't have confidence when talking to others then what follows is for you.

Here are some pointers on how to talk with confidence.

1. Slow down

Many people who lack confidence in talking with others will sometimes talk so fast when given an opportunity to talk that those who are listening quickly get lost in what is being said.

If you are talking too fast for people to understand you they will tune you out, and this will further damage your confidence in talking with others. To preserve what confidence you have, relax and talk at a moderate talking speed.

2. Practice speaking with confidence

Confidence is something we build with practice and experience. There is not one baseball pitcher ever born with the confidence of striking batters out. The pitcher had to practice and improve his skill and in that comes the confidence he needs to strike a skilled batter out.

Every chance you get, practice speaking with confidence. Talk to yourself in your mirror as if your reflection was another person.

3. Increase your vocabulary

Having a good verbal repertoire will help you talk with confidence because you are more flexible. And believe it or not, people who can clearly understand what's being said and then can clearly express themselves, are people that most people find interesting to be in a conversation with.

You can quickly and easily increase your vocabulary by committing to learn one new word a week. Take some time each week to read good fiction and you'll notice your vocabulary improving.

4. Look into their eyes

If you lack confidence in talking to anyone, don't show it. One of the best ways you can do this is by looking into the other person's eyes when either of you are talking, even if you don't feel confident inside.

Looking into the eyes of the person you are talking to says you are sincere and confident. When someone doesn't look you in the eye while talking with you it could indicate shame or that they have something to hide.

Don't give that impression to anyone.

5. Watch the red flags

There are red flags that can send a message to the other person that you don't have confidence.

The questions, "You know?" and "Right?" are two examples of red flags of a person who doesn't have confidence and needs to hear the other person's affirmations. In the business world those two are unprofessional, and in severe cases, very annoying.

6. Feel confident

Let yourself experience the feelings of confidence in those moments that you are feeling confident. Your confidence can be built and reinforced best when you can see it and experience it. There's a saying somewhere that indicates if you act confident you will become confident. There is much truth in that.

There are many people who need confidence, or more of it, when talking with other people. Following these points will help you to talk with greater confidence.

How to Talk to New People

It is always good to meet new people, who will hopefully turn into friends, but sometimes making conversation with someone you have just met can be rather intimidating, particularly if you are a bit shy or reserved. That is why it is important to learn how to talk with new people.

1. Don't just be a wallflower, and try to camouflage yourself against the wallpaper so that nobody will notice you the next time you go to a party: make an effort and join in with the fun.

Those other people are only human, just like you, and you could be missing out on meeting either the partner of your dreams, or at least a good friend to go out with, if you let your fears and inhibitions get the better of you.

2. If you are not sure how to start up a conversation with a stranger, try to listen to other people's conversations, and see how they do it (be subtle about this, though, as you don't want to get a reputation as an eavesdropper).

If you spot someone at a party or conference that you think would be pleasant or interesting to talk to, take a deep breath, go over and smile, and say, 'Hi.' Make a general comment about the event that you are attending to break the ice, and introduce yourself.

You could perhaps offer to help them to food or drink. Holding a glass gives you something to do with your hands, too.

3. If you are shy, or not very adept at social conversations, you might find it easier to join in a group conversation, rather than chatting in a one on one situation, since then you will not have to take as much responsibility for maintaining the flow of conversation.

If you already know one or two members of the group, it is even better, as this will help you to overcome your shyness with the ones that you don't know. If it makes you feel more comfortable, you can stand on the sidelines and just listen at first, and then gradually join in with the conversation as you become more confident.

4. Stick to general, innocuous topics, and avoid controversial subjects such as politics and religion. You could ask the other person if they have seen a film or TV show that you have recently watched; talk about a prominent sporting event that is currently in the news, or even chat about the weather. Ask them where they live and what they do for a living; whether they are married, or have any children or pets.

By asking questions like these, you show that you are interested in them, and, since most of us quite like talking about ourselves, they will be flattered and feel well disposed towards you.

Try not to ask closed questions, to which people can simply answer 'yes' or 'no', but pose open questions that require them to give a fuller response. This will help to keep the conversational ball rolling.

5. Make sure that you pay attention to what the other person is saying. Smile and nod so that they know that you are listening.

Once you begin to learn a little bit about the other person, you will have a better idea of their interests, and their attitudes towards life, and this will give you clues about the topics that are more likely to successfully sustain the flow of conversation.

Hopefully, you will find at least one issue or interest that you have in common, which will then make it much easier to find things to say.

For most of us, learning how to talk to new people is not easy, but you will find that the more practice you get, the better at it you will become.

How to Deal with Loneliness

We have all had to deal with loneliness at one time or other. No person is immune to feeling lonely. People with everything they could ever dream of have felt lonely just like the person with nothing has.

Loneliness also can come upon us at anytime and anywhere we might be. We can be in a very crowded place and feel lonely just as we might when we are the only person in a room.

However, there are some techniques you can use to help you. Here is a short list of strategies to deal with loneliness.

1. Change where you are at

One possible way to deal with loneliness is to move from where you are experiencing this emotion. If you live alone, for example, and feel lonely, get out of the house and maybe take a stroll down a busy city sidewalk.

As you pass people, try to connect with them with eye contact and a smile. Most people will smile back and this reciprocal connection may be the antidote to your loneliness.

Also, being of service to others, like at a food pantry or soup kitchen, can help you feel useful. When you feel useful you will feel connected. Often a lack of human connection can arouse the feeling of loneliness, so doing something useful for someone else can help to reduce your loneliness.

2. Change who you are around

There will be times when you are around people you just can't seem to relate to. This happens to many people, especially at social events and gatherings. You could be standing amongst a group of people that you just can't seem to click with.

You stand there just nodding your head with a blank stare on your face because you can't relate and connect with them. This can cause you to feel lonely. When this kind of situation occurs, politely withdraw yourself and seek another person or group to become involved with.

3. Switch your perspective

Factually speaking, loneliness is all in the mind. Again, loneliness is an emotion and is not an object outside of you. Therefore, it becomes possible to change it by changing the perception of how you are viewing loneliness.

One way to do that is to consider that other people are experiencing the same thing at the same moment you are. Looking through your loneliness towards another's will ground you and help you feel more human because now your loneliness becomes a shared experience.

4. Take relational risks

Loneliness is all about you and your perception of our loneliness. But part of that perception is also about how you see your relational abilities. That is, if you believe you can't relate to others and them to you then you just isolated yourself from connecting with anyone.

Everyone has something in common with someone else that will help you make a connection with them. There is someone in the world somewhere that you can connect with and them with you. And the way to find that connection is to let go of your faulty perception of loneliness and take a risk in allowing yourself to find that person you can connect with.

Dealing with loneliness is all a matter of perception and how you think and react to loneliness. Every human being experiences this emotion at some point in their lives. It's unavoidable because it's part of human nature. But what you do with it, or react to it, is what will make all the difference in the world to how your life will be affected by it. The choice is yours to make.

How to Talk to Strangers

Unless you are a particularly self confident person, talking to strangers is something that is likely to make you feel a bit nervous, but this is a problem that can be overcome with a little effort.

1. Practice makes perfect

The more that you talk to strangers, the easier it will become. You can start off in a small way. For example, if you are waiting at the bus stop, pluck up courage and make an innocuous remark about the weather, or the unreliability of the bus service, to the person standing next to you. It is very unlikely that you will meet with a rebuff.

Then, keep on practicing; pass a friendly comment to the supermarket cashier, the clerk at the bank and the receptionist at the doctor's surgery, rather than just stating your business.

Taxi drivers and hairdressers are usually notorious for chatting to their customers, so instead of ignoring or rebuffing them, use it as another practice session. By doing this, your confidence will increase in leaps and bounds, and you will find it easier each time that you do it.

2. Approach new people

At parties, conferences or other social events, if you cannot immediately see anyone that you know, instead of hiding in a corner, try to make some new acquaintances.

Look out for someone else who is standing on their own, and if they look approachable, go over and start a conversation. If you don't feel that you can walk up to them just like that, take over a tray of nibbles as an excuse, introduce yourself, and then you can strike up a chat.

Always begin with small talk, such as, 'Isn't this a lovely room?' or 'It's a good turnout, isn't it?' This will not make the other person feel threatened, and will give them an opening for something to say back to you.

3. Keep the conversation flowing

To sustain the conversation, you will need to keep a flow of questions and answers going, particularly if the other person is shy too. Don't get too personal at first, but you can discuss films and TV programs, sporting events, music and so on.

Later on, if things go well, you can then ask about their job, family etc. Listen attentively to what the other person has to say, and don't interrupt or talk over them. Smile, nod and make eye contact with them to show that you are interested in what they have to say.

4. Move on if there is no rapport

If you find that you have nothing in common with the other person, that they are unbearably boring, or have nothing much to say for themselves, find a polite excuse to terminate the conversation. This can be something along the lines of, 'Oh, I'm sorry, do excuse me, but I've just spotted my friend Sarah over there, and I really have to talk to her. It has been lovely chatting with you.' That way, you won't hurt their feelings.

5. Ease into group conversations

It can be even more difficult if you find yourself having to chat with a whole group of strangers, for example during a break at a conference.

If you feel nervous, try to stand on the outskirts of the group at first and listen to what the others have to say, until you feel confident enough to join in with the conversation.

In this situation, the obvious topic of conversation will be the content and presentation of the conference itself, so if you have been paying attention, you are just as well equipped to talk about this as any of the other delegates. Think about what you are going to say, rather than just blurting something out, and that way you are less likely to risk making a fool of yourself.

Talking to strangers is intimidating at times, but with practice your self confidence will grow and you will gradually find that it is easier and easier to do. Remembering that the other person is probably just as shy and nervous as you can also be a big help.

Printed in Great Britain
by Amazon.co.uk, Ltd.,
Marston Gate.